Best Bike Rides
Albuquerque and Santa Fe

Help Us Keep This Guide Up to Date

Every effort has been made by the authors and editors to make this guide as accurate and useful as possible. However, many things can change after a guide is published—roads are detoured, phone numbers change, facilities come under new management, and so forth.

We welcome your comments concerning your experiences with this guide and how you feel it could be improved and kept up to date. While we may not be able to respond to all comments and suggestions, we'll take them to heart, and we'll also make certain to share them with the authors. Please send your comments and suggestions to the following address:

Globe Pequot
Reader Response/Editorial Department
246 Goose Lane
Guilford, CT 06437

Or you may e-mail us at:
editorial@falcon.com

Thanks for your input, and happy riding!

Best Bike Rides
Albuquerque and Santa Fe

The Greatest Recreational Rides
in the Area

JD & EMILY TANNER AND
SHEY LAMBERT

FALCONGUIDES

GUILFORD, CONNECTICUT
HELENA, MONTANA

An imprint of Rowman & Littlefield
Falcon, FalconGuides, and Outfit Your Mind are registered trademarks of Rowman & Littlefield.

Distributed by NATIONAL BOOK NETWORK

British Library Cataloguing-in-Publication Information Available

Library of Congress Cataloging-in-Publication Data

Tanner, J. D.
  Best bike rides Albuquerque and Santa Fe: a guide to the greatest recreational rides in the area / JD Tanner, Emily Ressler-Tanner.
    pages cm. — (Best bike rides series)
  Includes index.
    ISBN 978-0-7627-8289-5 (paperback) — ISBN 978-1-4930-1425-5 (e-book)
  1. Bicycle touring—New Mexico—Albuquerque Region—Guidebooks. 2. Bicycle touring—New Mexico—Santa Fe Region—Guidebooks. 3. Santa Fe Region (N.M.)—Guidebooks. 4. Albuquerque Region (N.M.)—Guidebooks. I. Ressler, Emily. II. Title.
  GV1045.5.N62T36 2015
  796.6'409789—dc23
                          2015001133

∞™ The paper used in this publication meets the minimum requirements of American National Standard for Information Sciences—Permanence of Paper for Printed Library Materials, ANSI/NISO Z39.48-1992.

Contents

🏔 Road Bike   🚵 Mountain Bike   🚲 Hybrid

Albuquerque Metro Area

East of Albuquerque

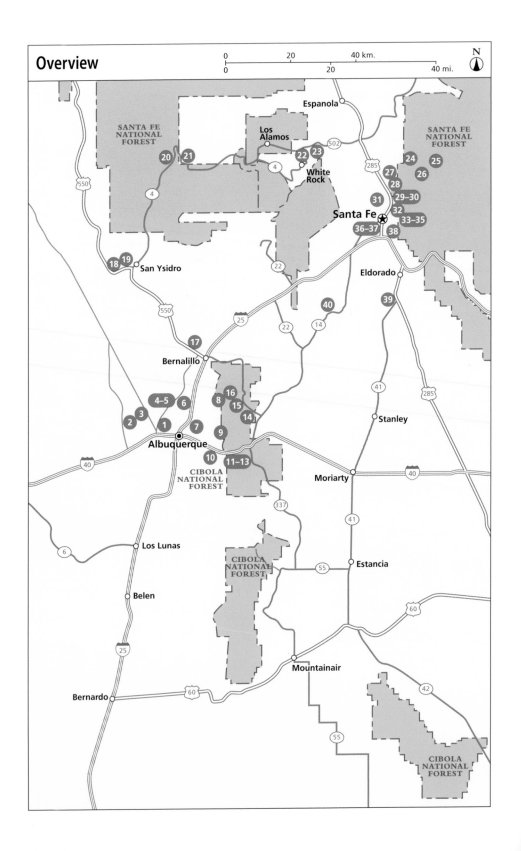

Acknowledgments

We would like to thank all those who helped us with the rides and information found in this guide. From land managers to friends to folks we met on the trails, we appreciate your expertise and willingness to help us make this the best possible biking guide.

We would like to give a special thanks to our family and friends Janet Wade, Aspen, and Zoey Wren, who joined us on several of the rides in this guide. Your company was very much appreciated! We'd also like to thank Catherine Smith, Vicki Miller, Lynn Spence, Rebecca Knack, Lauren Hale, Kayla Quintero, Sarah Rubow, Kelsey Frazzini, Sheena Ross, and Bruce Cline. Your guidance in finding good trails and good restaurants was much appreciated.

Finally, we would like to thank all our friends at Falcon Guides, particularly Imee Curiel and Meredith Dias, for their support and encouragement, and for making a book out of our rough manuscript.

We hope you enjoy riding the trails in this guide as much as we do!

Introduction

Welcome to New Mexico, the "Land of Enchantment." Whether you were born here, imported here, or merely visiting the state, you will find unique landscapes with an abundance of natural wonders and rich cultural experiences. Rocky summits, wild rivers, high-mountain deserts, and powdery slopes keep even the most active outdoor enthusiast busy here.

Situated in the "Heart of New Mexico" are the cities of Albuquerque and Santa Fe. Combined, these two cities make up over 30 percent of the state's total population. While unique in many ways, what these two cities have in common is an abundance of bike trails. A bike guide to either city would be well worth the money. Considering that Albuquerque and Santa Fe are only an hour apart, it is easy to say that this area is easily one of the best locations for riding in the country. Even the most energetic of bikers will struggle to see all this area has to offer.

Albuquerque is the state's largest city and only metropolitan area. Named "One of the Best Cities for Outdoor Adventure" by *National Geographic Adventure* magazine, Albuquerque serves as the jumping-off point to many of the state's finest adventures. One would be hard pressed to find another city with such easy trail access—the Sandia Mountains are literally in the city's backyard.

Santa Fe is the fourth-largest city in New Mexico and the state's capital. It holds the distinction of being the oldest capital city in North America. Spanish settlement dates back to 1607—that's thirteen years before the Pilgrims settled at Plymouth! At 7,000 feet, the city also is the highest capital in the United States. It's a dream come true for those who consider themselves "outdoorsy." In fact, it's so outdoorsy that *Outside Magazine* calls the city home.

This guidebook will show you some of the best trails that Albuquerque, Santa Fe, and the surrounding areas have to offer. Whether you are visiting the Land of Enchantment or just exploring your own hometown (lucky dog), you will be surprised by the variety of trails in this spectacular area.

In this guide we've selected easy, moderate, and more challenging rides near the cities of Albuquerque and Santa Fe that can meet the needs of new

> As the cities of Albuquerque and Santa Fe continue to grow, their parks, trails, and open spaces will become even more important. Recent studies have linked access to natural environments with lower crime rates, stress reduction, and health benefits for both children and adults.

and veteran riders alike. Some of the trails can be found within the city; others require a day trip to the surrounding areas. A variety of rides and terrain are profiled—road rides, paved paths, and rugged mountain trails. We have done our best to include a little of something for everyone: rides suited for families, for mountain bikers, for road riders, and for those seeking scenic views. Consider this an introduction to the area and a starting point to continue your New Mexico explorations—the ultimate sampler platter for biking in Santa Fe and Albuquerque. We have also tried to include some areas of interest near several of the trails to give visitors a chance to fully appreciate the unique areas included in this guide.

ALBUQUERQUE AND SANTA FE NATURAL AND CULTURAL HISTORY

Albuquerque and Santa Fe trails range from rugged and hilly to flat and paved. Rides in this guide cover a little bit of everything. While most of the trails in this guide can be ridden by most people and pose little threat to the rider, knowing a few details about the nature of the Albuquerque and Santa Fe areas will only enhance your explorations.

Natural History

It has taken hundreds of millions of years for the forces of nature to sculpt the landscape of New Mexico. Very few places can compare to New Mexico's diverse geography. Here you will find everything from the low desert plains in the south to the high Rocky Mountains in the north.

Although present-day New Mexico is thousands of feet above sea level, during the prehistoric Triassic, Jurassic, and Cretaceous periods, an ocean covered most of the state. When looking at the dry desert landscapes, rugged peaks, and impressive mountain vistas, it is hard to imagine the giant ocean that once covered this land, but fossil records tell the story of the early sea creatures that once flourished here.

Fossil records also show that this tropical climate created an ideal environment for dinosaurs. During the Cenozoic period, the ocean waters dried up and tectonic movement created the Rocky Mountains that are found here today.

New Mexico is also well known for its fascinating record of volcanic activity. Formations such as Ship Rock and Cabezon Peak are eroded remnants of ancient volcanoes. Valles Caldera National Preserve (www.vallescaldera.gov), located northeast of Albuquerque in the Jemez Mountains, is home to one of the largest calderas on earth. Evidence of eruptions from this giant volcano have been found as far north as Idaho and as far east as Kansas! Evidence of volcanic activity can even be seen from within the city of Albuquerque, as several remnants of cinder cone volcanoes are evident on the horizon of the West Mesa.

Mountain ranges in the area, including the Sandia, Manzano, and Sangre de Cristo Mountains, are the result of seismic activity.

Other natural wonders in the state include White Sands National Monument, the world's largest gypsum dune field, and Carlsbad Caverns National Park, home to over 110 limestone caves.

Common Flora and Fauna

New Mexico's altitude affects both the plant and animal life here. Due to its varied geology, six of the seven life zones are represented in the state. Because of this, the state has a diverse mix of both flora and fauna. Rides in

Dinosaurs in New Mexico

Those interested in learning more about the dinosaurs of New Mexico should make a point to visit Ghost Ranch, near Abiquiú. The Ruth Hall Museum of Paleontology is located on the ranch. Here you will learn about coelophysis (SEE-low-FY-sis), New Mexico's State Fossil, a tiny dinosaur that once roamed this beautiful ranch. For more information call (505) 685-4333, ext. 4118, or visit www.ghostranch.org/museums-and-activities/dinosaurs.

this guide take you through the Lower Sonoran, Upper Sonoran, Transition, and Canadian life zones.

The Lower Sonoran life zone, areas below 5,000 feet, describes most of southern New Mexico. This area supports cholla and prickly pear cactus, yucca, as well as mesquite, valley cottonwood, olive, and cedar trees. Desert foxes, kangaroo rats, antelope, roadrunners, and squirrels are common here, as are rattlesnakes, scorpions, centipedes, and tarantulas.

Many of the major mountain ranges in the state represent the Upper Sonoran life zone, from 5,000 to 7,000 feet in elevation. Many of the rides in this guide are found in this zone. Some of the plants and animals found in the Lower Sonoran zone are also found here. Additionally you will find juniper, piñon pines, oak, and sagebrush. Deer, coyotes, prairie dogs, and antelope are also found here. Mountain lions may be found in the higher elevations.

At 7,000 to 9,000 feet, much of north-central New Mexico is in the Transitional zone. Cooler temperatures provide habitat for mountain lions, black bears, elk, deer, quail, and wild turkeys. A wetter climate also provides more ideal habitat for ponderosa pine and Gambel oak. Many wildflowers can be spotted late spring through early fall.

Spruce, aspen, and fir trees can be found in the Canadian life zone (8,500–11,500 feet). Some trails in the Jemez region make their way into this zone. Deer, elk, chipmunks, and several species of squirrel find suitable summer habitats in this zone.

Areas above 11,500 feet are known as the Hudsonian zone and the Arctic-Alpine zone. These areas are home to bighorn sheep, yellow-bellied marmots, and American pikas. Some species of juniper and spruce, bristlecone pine, berry bushes, hardy grasses, and wildflowers grow here as well.

Cultural History

Although it did not become a state until 1912, New Mexico has an incredibly rich history that dates back to prehistoric times. Several of the rides in the guide travel near areas of cultural significance.

The Highs and Lows

The lowest point in New Mexico, 2,842 feet above sea level, is located at the northern end of the Red Bluff Reservoir on the Pecos River.

Wheeler Peak, the highest point in New Mexico, is 13,161 feet above sea level. It is located near Taos in the Sangre de Cristo Mountains.

Evidence found in Sandia Man Cave, located near several of the trails in this guide, shows the first known people to live in New Mexico were big-game hunters who came here between 12,000 and 8,000 years ago. They are known as the Clovis and Folsom peoples. Most of what is known about these people comes from the spear points they left behind. Archaeologists have also uncovered animal remains at kill sites and believe these people hunted such big game as mammoth and mastodon.

People known as the Anasazi occupied the area as early as AD 1. "Anasazi" is a Navajo word that has been variously translated to mean "ancient ones," "old ones," or "ancient enemies." Present-day descendants of the Anasazi—the Hopi, Zuni, and Puebloan peoples of New Mexico—prefer to call their ancestors "pre-Puebloan." The remains of this culture are scattered throughout the Colorado Plateau. Their name is derived from their finely woven baskets, and this early period of the culture is known as the Basketmaker period. As the Anasazi evolved from strictly hunting and gathering, they developed horticulture and became more sedentary. They also chipped stone for tools and crafted various woven articles, including sandals. During this period the Anasazi constructed slab-sided cists for storage and lived either in upright structures fashioned from wooden posts or in pit houses.

After about AD 700, the culture further evolved into what is called the Pueblo period. During this period, beginning about AD 900, the Anasazi population increased and they developed large villages in places. They became highly skilled at agriculture, and their ritualistic and social systems became well developed.

For reasons that may never be determined, the Anasazi began to build their dwellings and storage structures in nearly inaccessible, defensible positions high on the cliffs of the canyons. By the late 1200s the Anasazi had abandoned southern Utah and northern Arizona, and archaeologists theorize the abandonment may have occurred because of drought. Drought did occur in the mid-1200s, but why then did the Anasazi retreat still farther from scarce water into remote cliff dwellings during that time? Some archaeologists believe that warfare developed among the Anasazi in response to competition for dwindling resources. A newer theory suggests that the development of a new religion may have been responsible for the Anasazi abandonment of some regions and the move south and east into New Mexico and eastern Arizona.

Descendants of this ancient culture still live in houses of stone and mortar and today occupy the Hopi mesas in Arizona, the Zuni pueblo in western New Mexico, and numerous other pueblos scattered along the Rio Grande in northern New Mexico.

Protecting Cultural Sites

New Mexico's historical sites are nonrenewable resources offering archaeologists insights into past ways of life in the region, but they can be easily disturbed and damaged by careless visitors. Although federal and state laws protect cultural resources, ultimately it depends on each of us to walk (and ride) softly and treat these resources with the respect they deserve. Excavation and stabilization of many sites has yet to take place. Over-visitation is threatening many cultural sites in the region. Most people don't intentionally damage cultural sites, but having too many curious visitors often leads to site degradation. Leave all artifacts where you find them. Some people will take one or two arrowheads, thinking they will not be missed. Yet the cumulative effects of this practice lead to fewer signs of the Anasazi culture each year. Artifacts have much greater significance to all of us when observed in their original setting rather than gathering dust in a closet or on a mantle at home. Many well-intentioned visitors gather potsherds and other artifacts, placing them on display on so-called "museum rocks" at cultural sites. This may seem like a good idea, removing them from the ground where others may crush them, but removing artifacts from their resting place destroys clues needed by archaeologists gathering information about the site.

Skin oils easily destroy pigments of ancient pictographs. Restrain the urge to touch them, particularly handprint pictographs. Never add your own graffiti to irreplaceable rock art panels. Chalking, rubbing, tracing, and touching leads to the eventual disappearance of rock art and can make methods of dating panels impossible. Enjoy rock art by photographing, sketching, or viewing only.

Federal law protects these cultural sites, which are also places of great significance to Native Americans. These sites are preserved in what many have likened to an outdoor museum. Treat all sites you encounter as you would treat artifacts in any museum—with the care and respect that they deserve. The Antiquities Act of 1906 and the Archaeological Resources Protection Act of 1979 (ARPA) protect archaeological and historic sites. ARPA provides strong penalties, plus rewards for information leading to the arrest and conviction of vandals, pothunters, or others damaging protected sites. Notify Bureau of Land Management (BLM) managers or the county sheriff if you observe any illegal activity at cultural sites.

The descendants of the Anasazi are the Pueblo peoples, who have lived in and around the Sandia Mountains for thousands of years. Pueblo groups are distinguished from other native groups by many factors, but the one that gives Puebloans their name is their style of dwelling: adobe and stonework buildings organized into small towns, often defensive by design. Other groups that may be ancestors of the New Mexico Pueblo people are the Hohokam, a culture that reached its maximum in central Arizona, and the Mogollon culture, which thrived in and around the Mogollon Mountains in west-central New Mexico.

"Pueblo," the Spanish word for town, was the word the Spaniards used to describe the people they encountered while exploring the Southwest. Many of these people were farmers, and still are today. Although the Pueblo peoples shared a similar culture, they were not a single tribe. Even today the descendent of these Pueblo peoples speak different languages depending on which pueblo they come from. Pueblos near Albuquerque include Isleta Pueblo to the south, Laguna Pueblo to the west, and Sandia, Santa Ana, Zia, Jemez, San Felipe, Santa Domingo, and Cochiti Pueblos to the north.

In addition to the Pueblo peoples, other Native American tribes also live in New Mexico. The largest tribes of non-Pueblo peoples are the Apache and the Navajo. The exact date that the Navajo and the Apache tribes reached New Mexico is not known, but many archaeologists think it's sometime between the 1200s and 1500s. They may have been partly responsible for the abandonment of several Anasazi cliff dwelling and pueblos.

Today there are more than 270,000 Navajo people, making them the largest Native American tribe in the United States. The main Navajo reservation encompasses over 16 million acres of land in Arizona, New Mexico, and Utah. About one-third of the Navajo population lives in New Mexico.

Spanish conquistadors arrived in the settlements that would eventually become Albuquerque and Santa Fe in the mid to late 1500s. Later, in the 1600s, Spanish missionaries arrived and built missions here. In 1609 New Mexico became a royal colony of Spain. European diseases had devastating effects on the Pueblo peoples in the area, and by the mid-1600s Spanish farmers had established several farms in the valley. During this period the Native Americans in the area were subject to much suppression, and in 1680 they rebelled against the Spaniards, killing many and driving the rest out of the valley.

The Native Americans held Albuquerque for the next twelve years, at which point the governor of New Mexico, Diego de Vargas, reestablished Spanish control of the Rio Grande Valley. In 1706 King Philip of Spain allowed the colonists to establish Villa de Albuquerque.

New Mexico continued under Spanish rule until 1821, when New Spain (present-day Mexico) won its independence from Spain. In 1821 New Mexico became part of the "new" nation of Mexico.

After the Mexican-American War, New Mexico became a territory of the United States in 1850. It remained a territory for over sixty years before finally becoming a state in 1912.

As you can tell, the culture of New Mexico has been greatly shaped by all who have lived here. Native American, Spanish, Mexican, and American traditions are alive and well in the state today.

WEATHER

One of the sunniest cities in the United States, Albuquerque receives a whopping 310 days of sunshine each year; Santa Fe isn't far behind, with 283 sunny days a year. The mild, dry climate combined with very low humidity creates ideal conditions for a variety of outdoor adventures.

Summers tend to be warm and dry. While daytime highs average 90°F (32°C), locals say it's a "dry heat," and the low humidity truly does make the heat much more tolerable, particularly if you can find shaded areas.

Winters tend to be mild. Snowstorms do strike on occasion, but snow rarely lasts for more than a day or two in the cities. Expect snow-covered trails in the surrounding mountainous areas throughout winter. Skiing and snowshoeing trails can be found in the nearby mountains.

Fall and spring are particularly enjoyable in central New Mexico. Daytime highs hover around the mid-70s for much of the year.

Weather Averages for Albuquerque

Month	Average High (Fahrenheit)	Average Low (Fahrenheit)	Precipitation (Inches)
January	46	26	0.38
February	53	30	0.50
March	61	36	0.57
April	69	43	0.61
May	79	53	0.50
June	88	62	0.66
July	90	67	1.50
August	87	65	1.58
September	81	58	1.08
October	69	46	1.02
November	56	34	0.57
December	46	27	0.50

(Statistics from the Weather Channel, June 2014)

Weather Averages for Santa Fe

Month	Average High (Fahrenheit)	Average Low (Fahrenheit)	Precipitation (Inches)
January	44	18	0.60
February	48	22	0.55
March	56	26	0.94
April	65	32	0.77
May	74	41	0.94
June	84	49	1.29
July	86	55	2.33
August	83	53	2.23
September	78	47	1.54
October	67	36	1.33
November	53	25	0.85
December	43	18	0.83

(Statistics from the Weather Channel, June 2014)

No matter the season, be prepared for dramatic temperature shifts from day to night. Also note that the temperature averages listed below are for the cities of Albuquerque and Santa Fe. Many of the rides in this book are located in mountainous areas; expect dramatically lower temperatures at higher elevations.

LEAVE NO TRACE

Most people who enjoy outdoor activities naturally want to take care of the places they visit. If you are reading this book, you are probably one of those people. By following the Leave No Trace principles, you can ensure the continued care of the places you love to visit and preserve these areas for future generations.

You are encouraged to carefully plan your trip so that you know as much as you possibly can about the area you will be visiting. Weather forecasts, trail conditions, and water availability are just a few important factors to consider when planning a successful trip.

Once you begin your ride, do your best to stick to trails so that you do not inadvertently trample sensitive vegetation. Be prepared to pack out anything you bring in with you, and it never hurts to carry out trash others may have left behind. Be extra careful when visiting sites of historical and natural importance. Leave everything as you found it, and never remove artifacts found in these sensitive areas. The old saying "Take only photos, leave only footprints" goes a long way here in New Mexico.

Consider your impact on wildlife as you visit their homes, and be sure not to feed any wild animal; this act is unhealthy for wildlife and dangerous for people. Respect other visitors and users as well by keeping your pets on a leash, moving to the side of the trail to let others pass, and keeping noise to a minimum.

For more information on enjoying the outdoors responsibly, please contact the Leave No Trace Center for Outdoor Ethics at (800) 332-4100 or visit their website at www.LNT.org.

POSSIBLE HAZARDS

While some of the rides in this book are just minutes from the cities of Albuquerque and Santa Fe, others are in remote areas that may present hazardous conditions. Unexpected injury or illness, extreme heat, heavy rains or snow, flash floods, lack of water, dehydration, and encounters with venomous creatures or spiny cacti can all stop you in your tracks.

Conditions are constantly changing, so always obtain up-to-date information on trails, routes, road conditions, and water availability from the land management agencies listed in this guide. Before you leave home, let a family member, a friend, or an employer know where you are going and when you plan to return. Make arrangements so that if you do not return home or make contact by a certain time, that person can initiate search-and-rescue operations. Upon returning from your trip, be sure to notify that person to avoid an unnecessary search. Always sign trailhead registers where available. Information from trailhead registers has helped locate and save several overdue riders.

Flash floods are always a danger to be reckoned with, and as little as 0.25 to 0.5 inch of rain falling in a short period can result in a newborn stream coursing down a dry wash. A moderate rain lasting 2 to 3 hours can result in a significant flash flood. During the summer monsoon season (generally mid-July through mid-September) torrents of rain are unleashed from towering thunderheads in hit-and-miss fashion across the region.

Lightning often occurs with summer thunderstorms. Keep your eye on the sky; dark cumulonimbus clouds herald the approach of a thunderstorm. If one is approaching, stay away from ridges, mesa tops, the bases of cliffs, solitary trees, shallow overhangs and alcoves, and open areas. Seek shelter in thickets of brush or in piñon-juniper woodlands where the trees are plentiful, small, and of uniform size. Barring that kind of shelter, retreat to a boulder field or low-lying area. Keep in mind that, contrary to myth, lightning often strikes repeatedly in the same location.

The area also has its share of cacti, thorny shrubs, and biting insects that can injure you if you are careless. Biting flies and gnats are common throughout the region. Deerflies and sand flies are aggressive, carnivorous, and common in sandy areas of washes during the warmest months of the year, generally June through mid-September. Only during the cooler months will you encounter mosquitoes, and then usually only in limited numbers, primarily near water sources.

Various spiders (including the black widow and tarantula), scorpions, and centipedes inhabit the region. Scorpions are the most common. Most can inflict a painful sting, but their venom is rarely life threatening. Scorpions spend the day in the shade in dark crevices under rocks, logs, and bark. Be careful where you put your hands and feet, and avoid picking up rocks. Be careful at night and look before you sit.

Ants are also prevalent throughout the area. Red harvester ants can inflict a memorable sting, and tiny red ants may march toward your pack and food.

Several species of venomous snakes are found in New Mexico. Fortunately snakes pose a minimal threat to riders. Most snakebites are the result of people stepping on snakes or trying to pick them up, so leave them alone when you see them. Snakes rest in the shade to avoid midday heat, so use caution when stepping over logs and boulders, and watch where you put your hands and feet. Throwing rocks down a descending route can sometimes warn rattlesnakes of your presence.

30/30 Rule of Lightning

If there is less than 30 seconds between the time you see lightning and the time you hear thunder, you should take shelter indoors. If you cannot take shelter indoors, move to a safer location, away from trees, fences, and poles. Assume the lightning position and stay there for 30 minutes after the last flash of lightning.

Beware of the spines of cacti and yucca. Although cactus spines are painful, they can usually be removed with tweezers. The glochids—those tiny hairlike spines—are more difficult to remove and can cause painful irritation. Use adhesive tape to remove them, since probing with fingernails or tweezers often embeds them deeper into your skin.

Yucca plants have large, stiff spines that can inflict a painful puncture wound. If one of these spines breaks off in your hand, leg, or arm, it can be very difficult to remove, and you may have to endure the discomfort until a doctor can remove it.

Riders may encounter mountain lions and/or black bears on trails at higher elevations. Running into these animals is rare; attacks are even rarer. Trails that traverse mountain lion and black bear habitat are generally labeled. Recommendations for riding in black bear habitat and mountain lion habitat are very similar: Avoid riding alone, keep small children and pets close to you, and be aware of your surroundings. Never approach these animals, make yourself appear "bigger" if approached, and fight back if attacked. For more information on riding in mountain lion and black bear habitat, contact local land management agencies.

Finally, several of the trailheads in the Albuquerque and Santa Fe areas have had issues with vehicles being broken into and valuables being stolen. For this reason, we recommend not leaving any valuables in your vehicle while riding.

PLANNING THE RIDE

"Be prepared." The Boy Scouts say it, Leave No Trace says it, and the best outdoors people say it. Being prepared won't completely keep you out of harm's way when outdoors, but it will minimize the chances of finding yourself there. Here are some things to consider:

- Familiarize yourself with the basics of first aid (bites, stings, sprains, and breaks), carry a first aid kit, and know how to use it.
- Hydrate! No matter where or when you are riding, you should always carry water with you. A standard is 2 liters per person per day.
- Be prepared to treat water on longer rides. Untreated water from rivers and streams is not safe to drink in the Albuquerque and Santa Fe areas. Iodine tablets are small, light, and easy to carry.
- Carry a backpack filled with the "Ten Essentials": map, compass, sunglasses/sunscreen, extra food & water, extra clothes, headlamp/flashlight, first-aid kit, fire starter, matches, and knife.
- Pack your cell phone (set on vibrate as a courtesy to others) as a safety backup.

- Keep an eye on the kids. Have them carry a whistle, just in case.
- Get into riding shape before you head out! Note the length and difficulty of the trail, and match those factors with the experience and physical condition of those in your group. There are plenty of easy trails in this guide. If you are unsure where to begin, start easy and work your way up to more strenuous and lengthy pursuits.

TRAIL ETIQUETTE

There are many guidelines to take into consideration when learning good trail etiquette. Not only do bikers have a difficult time absorbing all these guidelines but other trail users do as well. An easy way to practice good trail etiquette is to think back to four things taught in kindergarten: "Sharing is caring"; "Treat everyone the way you want to be treated"; "Don't make a mess"; and "Have fun." These are simple yet rewarding lifelong lessons that can be applied to ensure that everyone has an excellent trail experience.

- **"Sharing is caring."** Depending on where you are, trails can be accessible to bikers, hikers, equestrians, and even motorized vehicles. So how do we share the trail? The general rules are as follows:
  - **Bikers:** Yield to all hikers, equestrians, and nonmotorized vehicles.
  - **Motorized vehicles:** Yield to everyone.
  - **Everyone:** Yield to equestrians.
  - **Special considerations:** Bikers traveling downhill should yield to bikers traveling uphill. Hikers traveling downhill should also yield to hikers traveling uphill. Also, make yourself known. Let hikers in front of you know you are behind them. Slow down, say hello, and ask if you may pass by. Don't scream "On your left!" This isn't a race. Besides, the person may not understand what you mean.
- **"Treat everyone the way you want to be treated."** Be considerate to wildlife and other trail users. Animals can be easily startled, and we are in their habitat. If you encounter an animal on or near the trail, slow down and give it time to adjust to your presence. Be friendly; smile, and say hello to every person you encounter along the trail. Remember that we are all stewards of the trail. It is our responsibility to make sure everyone enjoys his or her trail experience.
- **"Don't make a mess."** Keep the trails clean, don't litter, and stay on designated trails. Building your own trail can be fun, but if you want to do this, get a permit. Creating shortcuts on trails can cause erosion and may also affect animal habitats. If we don't all respect the land and keep the trails clean, we could lose out on opportunities for new trails in the future.

- **"Have fun."** Trails are a place we can escape to when we are having a rough time in our lives. Have fun out there; don't take life so seriously. Go play, act like a little kid, and explore some new trails. The more you do, the more you will discover something great within yourself—and you'll be a better biker because of it.

LAND MANAGEMENT RULES AND REGULATIONS

It is important to keep in mind that from the time this book is published to the time that you are reading it, some land management rules and regulations may have already changed. You are encouraged to always check for new and updated information about the area you plan to visit. See appendix A for contact information on the agencies that manage the public lands where the rides in this book are located.

USING MAP, COMPASS, AND GLOBAL POSITIONING (GPS) DEVICES

Almost all the trails in this guide are well maintained, and most are marked or blazed. Each ride includes a map that is designed to keep you on the right path. You may choose to use a more detailed topographical map, available at retail stores or online from the US Geological Survey (www.usgs.gov). Carry and know how to use a map and compass and/or a GPS device, particularly in wilderness areas and on more remote trails. These tools can help keep you from getting lost in the wilderness.

How to Use This Guide

This guide is designed to be simple and easy to use. Each ride is described with a map and summary information that delivers the trail's vital statistics, including length, terrain you will encounter, traffic and other hazards, and trail contacts. Directions to the trailhead are also provided, along with a general description of what you'll see along the way. A detailed route finder (Miles and Directions) sets forth mileages between significant landmarks along the trail.

Key to icons used in this edition:

Road Bike   Mountain Bike   Hybrid

GETTING TO THE TRAIL

Most of the trails in this guide can be approached from one of the two major interstates that run through Albuquerque and Santa Fe (I-25 and I-40) or by other major highways. Detailed directions from Albuquerque or Santa Fe to the trailheads are included in this guide. Google Maps provides excellent supplemental maps to aid you in finding your way.

HOW THE RIDES WERE CHOSEN

This guide describes trails that are accessible to almost every rider, whether visiting from out of town or a local resident. The rides are no longer than 50 miles round-trip, and most are considerably shorter. They range in difficulty from flat excursions in the immediate Albuquerque and Santa Fe areas, perfect for a family outing, to more challenging rides in the Sandia, Sangre de Cristo, and Jemez Mountains. While these trails are among the best, keep in mind that nearby trails, sometimes in the same park or in a neighboring open space, may offer options better suited to your needs.

Most of the trails in this guide are well maintained and fairly straightforward, but some are rugged and poorly marked. You should follow the maps closely and refer to written ride descriptions to confirm your course and direction, particularly when approaching trail intersections.

The accompanying trail maps provide information including basic topographical changes, key landmarks, and trail intersections. Map, compass, and GPS devices are not necessary for the majority of rides in this guide, but you may find that these devices enhance your experience while riding.

The majority of the trails in this guide serve multiple user groups. Hikers, bikers, and equestrians share many trails in the Albuquerque and Santa Fe areas. A few trails in this book allow off-road vehicles on all or parts of the trail. Please be aware of trail etiquette when sharing the path with others.

SELECTING A RIDE

When selecting a ride, keep the goals and fitness level of you and those in your riding group in mind. Do you want to just get out and enjoy nature? Do you want to get in a good workout? Do you want to immerse yourself in the history of the area? Figuring out what you hope to get out of a ride will help you choose the appropriate riding destination. Also be aware of the goals of others in your riding group. If you want to log some serious trail miles and your partner wants to photograph spring wildflowers, neither of you is likely to enjoy your time on the trail. When riding with others, it is a good idea to communicate individual goals before setting out.

It is also a good idea to keep individual fitness levels in mind when selecting a ride. You and those you ride with will enjoy the trail more if you select a ride that is challenging, but not too challenging.

Keep in mind that what you think is easy is entirely dependent on your level of fitness, weather and temperature, trail conditions, and the adequacy of your gear. Use the trail's length as a gauge of its relative difficulty—even if climbing is involved, it won't be too strenuous if the ride is less than 5 miles long. The Ride Finder lists "Best Mountain Bike Rides," "Best Rides with Children," "Best Road Rides," "Best Bike Path Rides," "Best Rides for Great Views," and "Best Rides for Nature Lovers." Use these categories as a jumping-off point when selecting a trail.

Approximate riding times are based on the assumption that on flat ground, most riders average 8 to 14 miles per hour. Adjust that rate by the steepness of the terrain (on average, add an extra hour for every 1,000 feet of elevation gain) and your level of fitness (subtract time if you're an aerobic animal and add time if you're riding with kids), and you have a ballpark riding duration. Be sure to add more time if you plan to picnic or take part in other activities like birding, photography, or nature study.

> ### Enjoy and Respect This Beautiful Landscape
> *As you take advantage of the spectacular scenery offered by the Albuquerque and Santa Fe areas, remember that our planet is very dear, very special, and very fragile. All of us should do everything we can to keep it clean, beautiful, and healthy, including following the tips you'll find throughout this book.*

Ride Finder

BEST MOUNTAIN BIKE RIDES

8 North Foothills Trail
11 Blue Ribbon, Gnasty, and Otero Canyon Trails Loop
12 Tunnel Canyon Trail
13 Coyote and Chamisoso Trails Loop
18 White Ridge Bike Trails Loop
23 Caja del Rio Trail
25 Borrego, Winsor National Recreation, and Bear Wallow Trails Loop
29 Chamisa Trail
32 Dale Ball North Trails
33 Dale Ball Central Trails
34 Dale Ball South–Camino Loop

BEST RIDES WITH CHILDREN

1 Aldo Leopold Forest Trail
2 Petroglyph National Monument Volcanoes Trail
7 Paseo del Nordeste Recreation Trail

BEST ROAD RIDES

10 Tijeras Trot
14 Sandia Crest Road
17 Jemez Dam Road
22 White Rock Visitor Center to Valles Caldera National Preserve
30 Hyde Park Road Summit
38 Old Santa Fe and Pecos Trails

BEST BIKE PATH RIDES

3 Paseo de la Mesa Recreation Trail
4 Paseo del Bosque Recreation Trail
6 North Diversion Channel Trail
36 Arroyo de los Chamisos Trail

BEST RIDES FOR GREAT VIEWS

9 South Foothills Trail
19 San Ysidro Trials Area Trail
20 East Fork Trail: Battleship Rock to Jemez Falls
26 Aspen Vista Trail
28 Big Tesuque Trail
35 Atalaya Mountain Trail
37 Santa Fe Rail Trail
40 Cerrillos Hills State Park Trails

BEST RIDES FOR NATURE LOVERS

5 Corrales Bosque Trail
15 Tree Spring Trail
16 10K and Ellis Trails Loop
21 East Fork Trail: East Fork Trailhead to Las Conchas Trailhead
24 Rio En Medio
27 Aspen Ranch Trail
31 La Tierra Loop
39 Galisteo Basin Preserve Trails

Map Legend

Transportation

90	Interstate
285	Featured US Highway
285	US Highway
14	Featured State Highway
14	State Highway
CR 12	County/Local Road
	Featured Bike Route
	Bike Route
	Featured Trail
	Trail/Dirt Road
	Railroad

Hydrology

	Reservoir/Lake
	River/Creek
	Spring

Land Use

	National Park/Forest
	State/Local Park

Symbols

1	Trailhead (Start)
17.1	Mileage Marker
→	Direction Arrow
★	Capital
◉	Large City
○	Small City/Town
+	Airport
‿	Bridge
†	Church
	Historic District
🏛	Museum
P	Parking
⊼	Picnic Area
▪	Point of Interest
	Restrooms
	Ski Area
	University/College
❓	Visitor Center
▲	Volcano/Peak

Albuquerque Metro Area

Paseo de la Mesa Recreation Trail (Ride 3)

The vibrant bike culture of the American Southwest shines in the Albuquerque Metro Area. With a vast network of bike pathways and multiuse trails spanning over 400 miles, the metro area makes Albuquerque one of the best cycling cities in the country. Among the most popular bike paths in the metro area is the Paseo del Bosque, which parallels the Rio Grande for 16 miles through the center of the city. If you are looking for a city where you can ride your bike to dinner then take off on smooth singletrack for dessert, the Albuquerque Metro Area is the place for you.

Aldo Leopold Forest Trail

Named for one of the pioneers of the modern conservation movement, the Aldo Leopold Trail offers great opportunities for wildlife viewing within the city limits of Albuquerque. The Aldo Leopold Forest Trail was dedicated in 2009 in honor of Aldo Leopold and his love of the Rio Grande and its valley.

Start: Rio Grande State Park Nature Center parking area

Length: 3.1-mile lollipop

Riding time: 30 minutes

Best bike: Mountain bike

Terrain and trail surface: Gravel and dirt parking at the beginning; gravel trail; wooden plank bridge crossing; paved trail

Traffic and hazards: Motor vehicles may be encountered while leaving and returning to the parking area; no motor vehicles are allowed on the trails except for maintenance and emergency vehicles.

Maps: USGS Los Griegos; trail map available at the nature center

Trail contacts: Rio Grande Nature Center State Park, 2901 Candelaria Rd. NW, Albuquerque 87107; (505) 344-7240; www.emnrd.state.nm.us/index.html

Special considerations: Parking lot gates are closed and locked at 5 p.m. The trails can be accessed from the Candelaria access path, just outside the park entrance, outside of park hours.

Getting there: From I-40 in Albuquerque, take exit 157A to Rio Grande Boulevard. Turn right (north) onto Rio Grande Boulevard NW and drive 1.4 miles to Candelaria Road NW. Turn left (northwest) onto Candelaria Road NW and drive 0.6 mile to the park entrance. Turn right into the park and the parking area. **GPS:** N35 7.819' / W106 41.031'

THE RIDE

This short and easy ride celebrates a leader in modern-day wildlife conservation. Aldo Leopold was a conservationist, forester, writer, and outdoor enthusiast. He may be best known for his collection of essays, first published in 1949, titled *A Sand County Almanac: And Sketches Here and There*, in which he discusses many of his ideas on conservation, including the "land ethic."

Bridge near Rio Grande Nature Center

Leopold was born in 1887 in Burlington, Iowa, where he developed an interest in nature at a young age. He spent many hours exploring the natural world that surrounded his boyhood home. This passion for the outdoors led him to the Yale Forest School, where he joined the first generation of professional foresters. In 1909 he graduated with a master's degree from that program and pursued a career with the newly established USDA Forest Service in Arizona and New Mexico. Within a few short years, he had been promoted to the position of supervisor for the Carson National Forest in New Mexico. He spent many years in New Mexico and left behind an impressive environmental legacy here, including creation of the Gila Wilderness near Silver City, which was the first officially designated Wilderness Area in the United States.

Leopold had a special place in his heart for the city of Albuquerque and was an advocate for its responsible growth. He met his wife, Estella, here, and they lived in a house near the Rio Grande. Serving as secretary of Albuquerque's chamber of commerce, Leopold promoted the creation of what would later become the Rio Grande Valley State Park. Leopold's vision and efforts also eventually led to the creation of the Rio Grande Zoological Park, Botanical Gardens, and Rio Grande Nature Center. He also founded the Albuquerque Wildlife Federation.

The access to the Aldo Leopold Trail begins on the northwest side of the Rio Grande State Park Nature Center. Follow the gravel trail south, back out of the parking area. Parking lot gates are locked at 5 p.m., and vehicles still in the lot will be locked in overnight. If you plan on being on the trail after 5 p.m., park outside the gates.

Turn right (west) at 0.1 mile after leaving the parking area onto the Candelaria biking and walking path and ride along the gravel trail that has chain-link fence on either side. At 0.2 mile turn right (northeast) onto the paved trail surface and continue northeast to the Rio Grande State Park Nature Center west side entrance. Turn left (northwest) at 0.4 mile to cross the bridge and then turn right (north) to ride up the ramp to the Paseo del Bosque Recreation Trail. Cross over the recreation trail, headed west, to pick up the Aldo Leopold Forest Trail on the other side. Continue northeast on this asphalt trail,

A good portion of the trail is paved.

passing through a wooded area consisting mostly of cottonwood trees, which are prevalent in the Rio Grande bosque.

At 0.7 mile come to a wooden rest bench and continue northeast on the asphalt path. Come to another rest bench at 0.9 mile. Just after this bench, the trail curves to the left (northwest) and a sand/dirt path splits off to the right (north). A sign here proclaims the trail ahead to be the "Aldo Leopold Forest Trail." Take this path toward the river.

Reach the bank of the Rio Grande at 1.1 miles. From here follow the river northeast. Interpretive signs on the life and work of Aldo Leopold begin here. This is also a great place to look for birds, particularly waterfowl. It is common to see sandhill cranes, Canada geese, and several species of ducks here during the winter months. Roadrunners, raccoons, beavers, and coyotes can also be found in the area.

At 1.2 miles the trail becomes quite sandy; continue northeast through the cottonwoods. Come to a fork in the trail at 1.4 miles and turn left (north) toward the river. At 1.6 miles the trail makes a sharp turn to the right (southeast) before coming to Montaño Boulevard. Shortly after, you will notice a spur trail breaking off to the east (this spur leads from Montaño Boulevard); stay right and continue south through the cottonwoods as the trail runs parallel to the Paseo del Bosque Recreation Trail for a short time.

At 2.1 miles return to the fork in the trail; bear left (southwest) and follow the trail back toward the asphalt trail. At 2.6 miles return to the asphalt trail; take the right fork (southwest) and follow it back to the Rio Grande State Park Nature Center. Cross the bridge and reach the parking area at 3.1 miles.

MILES AND DIRECTIONS

0.0 Start from the northwest side of the parking area, following the gravel trail south.

0.1 Turn right (west) onto the Candelaria biking and walking path.

0.2 Turn right (northeast) onto the paved trail surface and continue northeast to the Rio Grande Nature Center State Park west side entrance.

0.4 Turn left (northwest) to cross the bridge and then turn right (north) to ride up the ramp to the Paseo del Bosque Recreation Trail.

0.7 Come to a wooden rest bench; continue northeast on the asphalt path.

0.9 Turn right (north) onto the Aldo Leopold Forest Trail.

1.1 Reach the Rio Grande; turn right (northeast).

1.4 Come to a fork in the trail; bear left (north) toward the river.

1.6 Make a sharp turn to the right (southeast); shortly after a spur trail joins the main trail, stay right (south).

2.1 Complete the loop portion of the trail. Turn left (southwest).

2.6 Return to the asphalt trail. Turn right (southwest).

3.1 Cross the bridge and arrive back at the parking area.

RIDE INFORMATION

Local Attractions/Events
Rio Grande Nature Center State Park, 2901 Candelaria Rd. NW, Albuquerque; (505) 334-7240; www.emnrd.state.nm.us/SPD/riograndenaturecenter statepark.html
Tingley Beach, 1800 Tingley Dr. SW, Albuquerque; (505) 768-2000; www.cabq .gov/biopark/tingley

Local Bike Shops
Bikeworks Albuquerque, 2839 Carlisle Blvd. NE, Albuquerque; (505) 884-0341; www.bikeworksabq.com
Cycle Cave, Inc., 5716 Menaul Blvd. NE, Albuquerque; (505) 884-6607

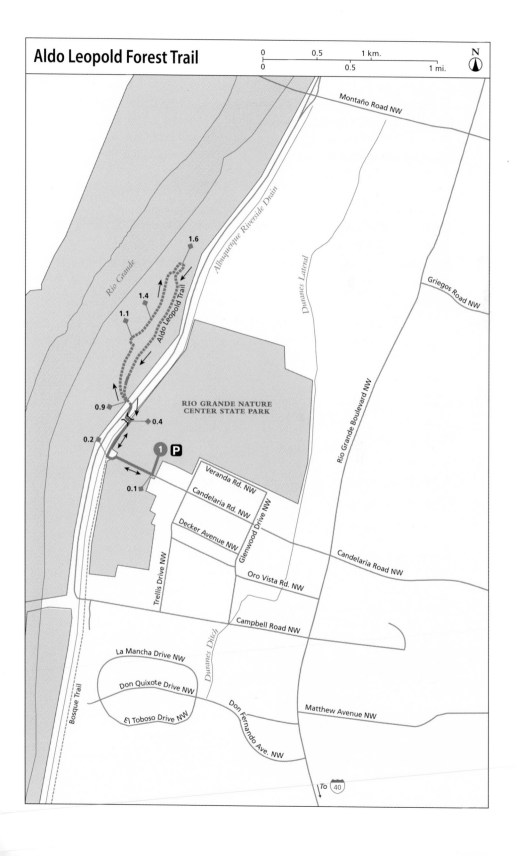

Aldo Leopold Forest Trail

0   0.5   1 km.

0   0.5   1 mi.

N

Montaño Road NW

Rio Grande

Albuquerque Riverside Drain

Duranes Lateral

Griegos Road NW

1.6

1.4

1.1

Aldo Leopold Trail

0.9

RIO GRANDE NATURE
CENTER STATE PARK

0.4

0.2

Rio Grande Boulevard NW

1 P

0.1

Veranda Rd. NW

Candelaria Rd. NW

Glenwood Drive NW

Decker Avenue NW

Candelaria Road NW

Trellis Drive NW

Oro Vista Rd. NW

Campbell Road NW

Duranes Ditch

La Mancha Drive NW

Don Quixote Drive NW

Bosque Trail

El Toboso Drive NW

Don Fernando Ave. NW

Matthew Avenue NW

To 40

Fat Tire Cycles, 421 Montaño Rd. NE, Albuquerque; (505) 345-9005; www.fat
tirecycles.com
Performance Bicycle Shop, 1431 Mercantile Ave. NE, Albuquerque; (505)
765-2471; www.performancebike.com
REI, 1550 Mercantile Ave. NE, Albuquerque; (505) 247-1191; www.REI.com
Sport Systems, 6915 Montgomery Blvd. NE, Albuquerque; (505) 837-9400;
www.nmsportsystems.com

Restaurants

El Patio De Albuquerque, 142 Harvard Dr. SE, Albuquerque; (505) 268-4245;
www.elpatiodealbuquerque.com
Monroe's, 6051 Osuna Rd. NE, Albuquerque; (505) 881-4224; www.monroes
chile.com
Range Café, 4401 Wyoming Blvd. NE, Albuquerque; (505) 293-2633; www
.rangecafe.com

Petroglyph National Monument Volcanoes Trail

Known by locals as the "Albuquerque Volcanoes" or the "Three Sisters," the sacred volcanoes sit just west of the city. From the city and even at a first close-up glance, this landscape appears to be a bit barren and much like the typical sagebrush-littered New Mexico desert. A closer look reveals that this nearly 3-mile ride covers area that provided the volcanic boulders found within the Petroglyph National Monument.

Start: Volcanoes day-use parking area, west of Albuquerque

Length: 2.8-mile double loop

Riding time: 30 minutes to 1 hour

Best bike: Mountain bike

Terrain and trail surface: Dirt and gravel trail; dirt road

Traffic and hazards: Motor vehicles may be encountered while leaving and returning to the parking area; no motor vehicles are allowed on the trails except for maintenance vehicles.

Maps: USGS Los Griegos; detailed trail map and brochure available at the Petroglyph National Monument visitor center

Trail contacts: Petroglyph National Monument, 6001 Unser Blvd. NW, Albuquerque 87120; (505) 899-0205; www.nps.gov/petr/index.htm

Special considerations: Severe weather can occur on the higher desert plains.

Getting there: From Albuquerque, take I-40 west to exit 149. Turn right (north) onto Atrisco Vista Boulevard and drive 4.8 miles to the unsigned Volcanes Access Road. Turn right (east) onto the road and drive 0.3 mile to the Volcanoes Day Use Area. **GPS:** N35 07.834' / W106 46.835'

THE RIDE

The Volcanoes Day Use Area in Petroglyph National Monument offers a unique opportunity to riders and other visitors. Today one of the few national park areas that allow mountain biking on the trails, it wasn't long ago that this area was used for military bombings, ranching, illegal dumping, and off-road vehicle use. Since the area was taken over by the National Park Service and the City of Albuquerque, the true beauty and amazing history of the area have been revealed and continue to unfold.

The Rio Grande Rift, which stretches from southern Colorado through New Mexico to Mexico, is one of only a few active rifts that exist in the world today. Basically, magma beneath the continent pushed the crust up, causing numerous cracks and fractures. These cracks and fractures weakened the area that is now the Rio Grande Rift Valley, causing it to collapse. The Sandia Mountains, which sit just east of Albuquerque, mark the eastern edge of the rift.

Within the rift, near Albuquerque, are the volcanic cones that sit on the West Mesa. Geologists believe that volcanic fissures occurred first and created the lava flows that left behind the volcanic escarpments in Rinconada and Piedras Marcadas Canyons. Later eruptions actually formed the volcanic cones that are still visible west of Albuquerque today.

The volcanoes that formed thousands of years ago and the petroglyphs that were pecked into the volcanic rocks hundreds of years ago are believed to be a sacred landscape to the Native Americans who live in this area today. They believe that these features are a spiritual connection to their ancestors as well as the Spirit World. The Pueblos, Navajo, and Apache believe this unique landscape was formed by ancient spiritual beings to help guide travelers on their quests.

From the Volcanoes Day Use Area parking lot, which has vault toilets and paved parking, bear right and begin riding southeast on the paved walkway/bike path that quickly becomes dirt, with JA Volcano in front of you. After just 0.1 mile you will come to a resting/viewing area on the right (south). Continue riding southeast and then east toward JA Volcano. At 0.4 mile a trail intersects from the left (north). This is the Black Volcano return loop trail. Continue

🍃 Green Tip
For rest stops, go off-trail so others won't have to struggle to get around you. Head for resilient surfaces without vegetation. Rock outcroppings and boulders are ideal.

View of Sandia Mountains from Volcanoes day-use area

straight (east) and ride along the north side of JA Volcano before reaching a scenic overlook at 0.5 mile.

At the scenic overlook turn left (north) and begin riding on the Black Volcano loop trail. The land appears barren, but if you really take the time to study the area, you will see all the life the desert has to offer. Dark basalt rock is all around, and sagebrush and other shrubs offer food and shelter to numerous small animals that live in the area.

After circling around the east side of Black Volcano, the trail curves northwest and connects with another trail at 0.9 mile. Stay right (north) onto the Vulcan Volcano loop trail. Left (south) will continue on the Black Volcano loop trail and return you to the parking area. Continue riding along the small saddle from Black Volcano to Vulcan Volcano. You will reach a trail junction at 1.3 miles, where you will want to stay right (north) and circle around Vulcan Volcano. The trail to the left (southwest) will return you to the parking area; take this trail after circling Vulcan Volcano.

Continuing north from the trail junction, the trail climbs steep rocky terrain to 1.5 miles. Turn right (northeast) here to loop around Vulcan Volcano. The trail around Vulcan is well traveled. The loop around Vulcan ends at 1.9 miles; you will need to descend the steep rocky terrain you climbed earlier.

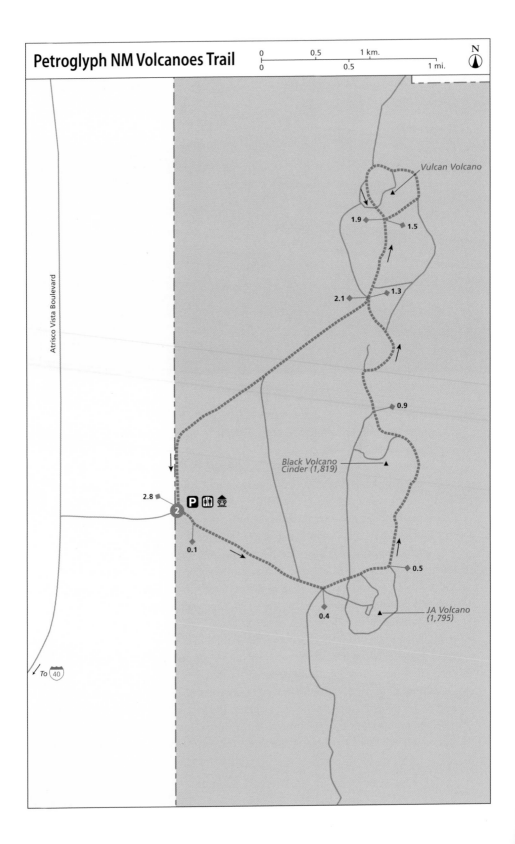

Petroglyph NM Volcanoes Trail

0   0.5   1 km.
0   0.5   1 mi.

N

Vulcan Volcano

1.9   1.5

2.1   1.3

0.9

*Black Volcano
Cinder (1,819)*

2.8

2

0.1

0.5

0.4

*JA Volcano
(1,795)*

Atrisco Vista Boulevard

To 40

Reach the trail junction for a second time after 2.1 miles; turn right (south-west), this time following the Vulcan Volcano return loop trail back to the parking lot. After a short ride through an open volcanic field, you will return to the north side of the parking area at 2.8 miles.

MILES AND DIRECTIONS

0.0 Start from the main trailhead sign and head right (southeast).

0.1 Come to a rest/viewing area on the right (south).

0.4 Reach the Black Volcano return loop to the left (north); continue riding straight ahead (east).

0.5 Come to a scenic overlook and the Black Volcano loop to the left (north). Turn left (north) onto the Black Volcano loop trail.

0.9 The Black Volcano loop connects with the Vulcan Volcano loop. Stay right (north) on the Vulcan Volcano loop.

1.3 The Vulcan Volcano loop meets the Vulcan Volcano return loop. Continue right (north) to loop around the Vulcan Volcano.

1.5 The loop around the Vulcan Volcano begins.

1.9 The loop around the Vulcan Volcano ends. Stay right (south) to continue to the Vulcan Volcano return loop.

2.1 Reach the Vulcan Volcano return loop trail and stay right (southwest) to return to the parking area.

2.8 Arrive back at the parking area.

RIDE INFORMATION

Local Attractions/Events

Petroglyph National Monument Visitor Center, 6001 Unser Blvd. NW, Albuquerque; (505) 899-0205; www.nps.gov/petr/index.htm

Shooting Range State Park, 16001 Shooting Range Access NW, Albuquerque; (505) 836-8785; www.cabq.gov/openspace/shootingrange.html

Local Bike Shops

The Bike Coop, 120 Yale Blvd. SE, Albuquerque; (505) 265-5170; www.bikecoop.com

The Bike Smith, 901 Rio Grande Blvd. NW, Albuquerque; (505) 242-9253; www.thebikesmith.com

Routes, Rentals, and Tours, 404 San Filipe St. NW, Albuquerque; (505) 933-5667; www.routesrentals.com

Trek Bicycle Superstore, 5000 Menaul Blvd. NE, Albuquerque; (505) 312-7243; www.trekbicyclesuperstore.com

Two Wheel Drive, 1706 Central Ave. SE, Albuquerque; (505) 243-8443; www.twowheeldrive.com

Restaurants

El Pinto Restaurant and Cantina, 10500 4th St. NW, Albuquerque; (505) 898-1771; www.elpinto.com

Frontier Restaurant, 2400 Central Ave. SE, Albuquerque; (505) 266-0550; www.frontierrestaurant.com

Taj Mahal, 1430 Carlisle Blvd. NE, Albuquerque; (505) 255-1994; www.tajmahalcuisineofindia.com

Paseo de la Mesa Recreation Trail

The Paseo de la Mesa multiuse trail has much to offer to the residents of Albuquerque and to biking enthusiasts visiting the area. Enjoy beautiful 360-degree views of the surrounding mountain ranges, including the Jemez, Santa Fe, Sandia, Manzano, San Mateo, and Magdalena Mountains, as well as such nearby peaks as Mounts Taylor, Ladron, and Polvadera.

Start: Northwest corner of the Paseo de la Mesa parking lot

Length: 8.4 miles out and back

Riding time: 1 to 2 hours

Best bike: Hybrid

Terrain and trail surface: Paved trail; gradual ascent out and fun, fast cruise back

Traffic and hazards: Motorized vehicles are not permitted on the trail except for maintenance and emergency vehicles. Riders may encounter hikers, walkers, runners, horses, and families.

Maps: USGS Los Griegos; detailed trail map and brochure available at the Open Space Visitor Center

Trail contacts: Open Space Division Parks and Recreation, 3615 Los Picaros Rd. SE, Albuquerque 87105; (505) 452-5200; www.cabq.gov/parksandrecreation/open-space/lands/paseo-de-la-mesa-trail

Special considerations: Severe weather and high winds can occur on the high-desert plains.

Getting there: From I-40 in Albuquerque, drive 5.4 miles on Unser Boulevard to Molten Rock Road. Turn left (west) onto Molten Rock Road and then left (south) again after just 0.1 mile onto 81st Street. Continue for 0.2 mile and then turn right (west) into the signed parking area for Paseo de la Mesa Recreation Trail. Stay right (northwest) on the one-way road to the parking lot. **GPS:** N35 15.824' / W106 72.932'

THE RIDE

The Albuquerque Major Public Open Space was developed to set aside land in the Albuquerque area to protect, maintain, and manage the cultural and natural resources. The program also provides outdoor education and recreational opportunities. The Albuquerque Open Space Visitor Center is considered the hub for the more than 29,000 acres of open space managed by the City of Albuquerque. The Open Space Division strives to educate the citizens of Albuquerque as well as visitors about the importance of protecting and preserving the lands in and around the city. The visitor center offers a number of exhibits, year-round educational programs, and even an art gallery.

The Paseo de la Mesa Recreation Trail is one of many trails managed by the Open Space Division, and the effort the city has put into these recreational opportunities has paid off for its residents. There are numerous riding opportunities around the city that locals can access for early-morning rides, lunchtime workouts, or quick getaways after work. Weekends can be very busy on

View of Sandia Mountains from Paseo de la Mesa Recreation Trail

Trail Etiquette

When you meet others on the trail, it can sometimes be a tricky social moment. Who has the right-of-way and who should step to the side? On trails that allow multiple users, such as hikers, bikers, and equestrians, the general rule of thumb is that hikers and bikers should yield to horses. Bikers yield to hikers. Following this etiquette can help all users have a safe and enjoyable experience on the trail.

the trails, so be prepared for some company if you plan on a Saturday or Sunday ride.

Locate the Paseo de la Mesa Recreation Trail at the northwest corner of the parking lot and begin riding northwest on the well-kept, paved trail. The trail quickly turns due west and begins a steady climb. You'll reach the end of a neighborhood on the right (north) and a trail access point at 0.4 mile, just before the trail gets a little steeper. Continue climbing as the beautiful volcanic and geologic features of the area begin to appear.

At 1.7 miles riders can look straight (west) ahead and catch great views of the Petroglyph National Monument Volcanoes Day Use Area. Here the trail makes a sharp right (north) turn and continues north. (Those looking for an adventure can ride west at the sharp turn and take the unsigned dirt trail to the volcanoes trails.) For this ride, continue riding north on the paved trail. Finally, after 2.5 miles of a steady climb, you get a brief downhill where you can quickly rest your legs before the climb begins again.

The trail makes a sharp left (west) turn at 3.1 miles and begins its final climb. Great views of the surrounding mountain ranges are to be had here. At 4.2 miles you reach the western access point for the trail and a less-developed parking area. Turn around here and return via the same route to the main trailhead parking area for a round-trip of 8.4 miles.

MILES AND DIRECTIONS

0.0 Start from the northwest corner of the parking area and begin riding northwest.

0.4 Pass a trail access point on the right (north).

1.7 The trail makes a sharp right (north) turn and continues north.

2.5 Enjoy a brief downhill section after a long gradual climb.

3.1 The trail makes a sharp left (west) turn.

Paseo de la Mesa Recreation Trail

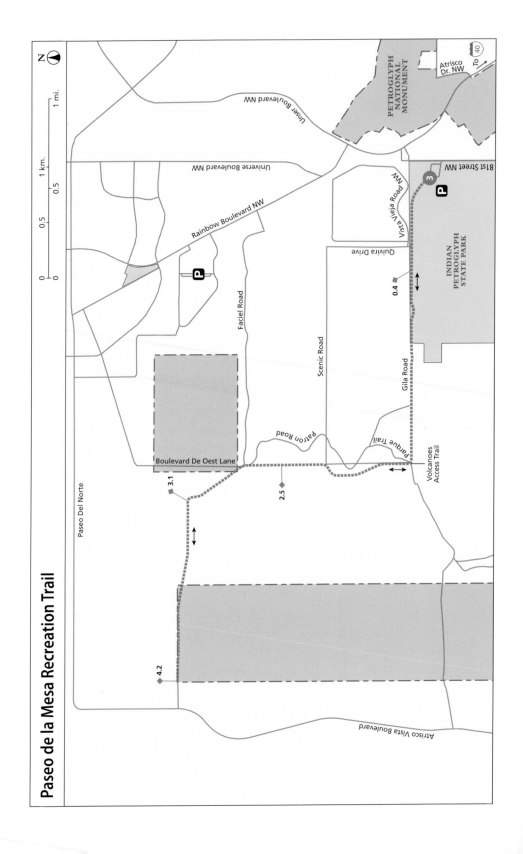

4.2 Reach the western trail access point and parking area. Return the way you came.

8.4 Arrive back at the trailhead parking area.

RIDE INFORMATION

Local Attractions/Events

Petroglyph National Monument Visitor Center, 6001 Unser Blvd. NW, Albuquerque; (505) 899-0205; www.nps.gov/petr/index.htm

Rio Grande Nature Center State Park, 2901 Candelaria Rd. NW, Albuquerque; (505) 344-7240, www.emnrd.state.nm.us/SPD/riograndenaturecenter statepark.html

Local Bike Shops

Bikeworks Albuquerque, 2839 Carlisle Blvd. NE, Albuquerque; (505) 884-0341; www.bikeworksabq.com

Cycle Cave, Inc., 5716 Menaul Blvd. NE, Albuquerque; (505) 884-6607

Fat Tire Cycles, 421 Montaño Rd. NE, Albuquerque; (505) 345-9005; www.fat tirecycles.com

Performance Bicycle Shop, 1431 Mercantile Ave. NE, Albuquerque; (505) 765-2471; www.performancebike.com

REI, 1550 Mercantile Ave., Albuquerque; (505) 247-1191; www.REI.com

Sport Systems, 6915 Montgomery Blvd. NE, Albuquerque; (505) 837-9400; www.nmsportsystems.com

Restaurants

El Patio De Albuquerque, 142 Harvard Dr. SE, Albuquerque; (505) 268-4245; www.elpatiodealbuquerque.com

Monroe's, 6051 Osuna Rd. NE, Albuquerque; (505) 881-4224; www.monroes chile.com

Range Café, 4401 Wyoming Blvd. NE, Albuquerque; (505) 293-2633; www .rangecafe.com

4

Paseo del Bosque Recreation Trail

The Paseo del Bosque multiuse trail has been mentioned in Sunset *and* National Geographic Adventure *magazines as one of the best urban trails in the West. Hikers, bikers, in-line skaters, and joggers all enjoy this 16-mile-long trail that has several access points. Riders should be on the lookout for beavers, numerous species of birds, snakes, and turtles along this 13.7-mile section (27.4 miles out and back).*

Start: Rio Grande Valley State Park parking area, south of Alameda Boulevard and east of the Rio Grande.

Length: 27.4 miles out and back

Riding time: 2 to 4 hours

Best bike: Hybrid

Terrain and trail surface: Paved

Traffic and hazards: No motorized vehicles are permitted on the recreation trail except for authorized and emergency vehicles. Hikers, runners, and equestrians also use the trail.

Maps: USGS Los Griegos; detailed trail map and brochure available at the Open Space visitor center

Trail contacts: Open Space Division Parks and Recreation, 3615 Los Picaros Rd. SE, Albuquerque 87105; (505) 452-5200; www.cabq.gov/openspace/riograndevalley.html

Special considerations: Be prepared to pack out trash from picnic areas and respect private property along the trail.

Getting there: From I-25 in Albuquerque, take exit 233. Turn left (west) onto Atrisco Alameda Boulevard NE/NM 528 and drive 3.4 miles to the Rio Grande Valley State Park parking area, on the left. **GPS:** N35 11.678' / W106 38.375'

THE RIDE

The Paseo del Bosque Trail, known by many locals as the Riverside Bike Path, is arguably the most popular and well-known trail within Albuquerque's city limits. The 16-mile-long multiuse trail runs along the Rio Grande through the middle of Albuquerque. The trail offers locals and visitors seven main accesses as well as numerous other access points. The trail is completely uninterrupted by roads or highways and regularly used by hikers, bikers, runners, skaters, and even horseback riders. That's right, horseback riders in downtown Albuquerque. Hey, it's the West!

Rio Grande Valley State Park is the starting point for this section of the Paseo del Bosque Recreation Trail. Try not to be fooled by the name though. Rio Grande Valley State Park isn't actually a state park. While the park was established by state legislature in 1983, it is managed by the City of Albuquerque Open Space and the Middle Rio Grande Conservancy District.

Locate the paved Paseo del Bosque Recreation Trail at the northwest corner of the Rio Grande Valley State Park parking lot. Turn left (south) onto the paved trail and continue south. The paved Paseo del Bosque trail parallels the Rio Grande and offers numerous areas to sit and rest. The cottonwoods that grow along the bosque offer plenty of shade for those hot summer desert days.

After 1.1 miles you pass under Paseo Del Norte NW and continue riding south. A nice view of the Rio Grande appears to the west through the cottonwoods at 2.5 miles. Beyond the river you can see the Albuquerque Volcanoes on the western mesa. After taking in the scenery, continue riding south along the paved trail and cross under Montaño Road NW at 4.2 miles. Not long after crossing under the road you will see signs for the Aldo Leopold Forest on the right (west). Continue riding south along this busy trail section and pass the Rio Grande State Park Nature Center at 5.3 miles on the left (east). The nature center does not allow bike traffic.

Arrive at the Gail Ryba Memorial Bridge and the I-40 Trail at 7.1 miles and continue south, under I-40. After a short stretch of peace and quiet, a variety of attractions will begin popping up along the trail. The first, at 8.3 miles, is the Botanical Gardens on the left (east). Shortly after, you come to Rotary

What Is a Bosque?

"Bosque" is a Spanish word meaning "woods" or "forest." In the Southwest it generally refers to the green ribbon of land surrounding a river's floodplain, such as the Rio Grande Bosque.

Trail marker on Open Space Visitor Center trails

River Park at 8.5 miles, Tingley Beach and Train Station at 9.0 miles, and the Albuquerque Zoo at 9.7 miles. From the trail you can catch a few glimpses of the elephants.

Stay right to ride under Bridge Boulevard SW at 10.4 miles and prepare for a quick change of scenery. The trail quickly leaves the hustle and bustle of the downtown and tourist attractions and makes its way out into quiet fields. Continue riding for more than 3 miles until you reach Rio Bravo Blvd. SW at

13.7 miles. The trail continues south from here to complete a short loop. This description ends at Rio Bravo Boulevard SW. Turn around and return to the trailhead via the same route for a round-trip of 27.4 miles.

MILES AND DIRECTIONS

0.0 Start on the paved trail. Turn left (south) and continue riding south.

1.1 The trail crosses under Paseo Del Norte Northwest.

2.5 Come to a nice view of the Rio Grande and the Albuquerque Volcanoes to the right (west).

4.2 The trail travels under Montaño Road Northwest.

5.3 Pass the Rio Grande State Park Nature Center on the left (east).

7.1 Arrive at the Gail Ryba Memorial Bridge and the I-40 Trail; continue south, under I-40.

8.3 Pass the Botanical Gardens on the left (east).

8.5 Pass Rotary River Park.

9.0 Pass Tingley Beach and Train Station.

9.7 Pass the Albuquerque Zoo.

10.4 Stay right to ride under Bridge Boulevard SW.

13.7 Arrive at Rio Bravo Boulevard SW. Return the way you came.

27.4 Arrive back at the trailhead parking area.

RIDE INFORMATION

Local Attractions/Events

Balloon Fiesta Park, 5000 Balloon Fiesta Pkwy. NE, Albuquerque; (505) 821-1000; www.balloonfiesta.com

Rio Grande Nature Center State Park, 2901 Candelaria Rd. NW, Albuquerque; (505) 344-7240; www.emnrd.state.nm.us/SPD/riograndenaturecenterstatepark.html

Local Bike Shops

The Bike Coop, 120 Yale Blvd. SE, Albuquerque; (505) 265-5170; www.bikecoop.com

The Bike Smith, 901 Rio Grande Blvd. NW, Albuquerque; (505) 242-9253; www.thebikesmith.com

Routes, Rentals, and Tours, 404 San Filipe St. NW, Albuquerque; (505) 933-5667; http://routesrentals.com

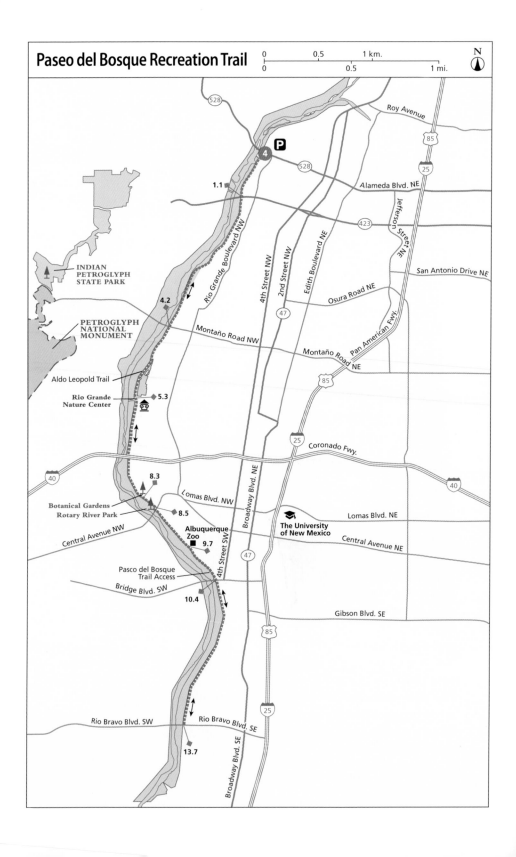

Paseo del Bosque Recreation Trail

N

Trek Bicycle Superstore, 5000 Menaul Blvd. NE, Albuquerque; (505) 312-7243; www.trekbicyclesuperstore.com

Two Wheel Drive, 1706 Central Ave. SE, Albuquerque; (505) 243-8443; www.twowheeldrive.com

Restaurants

El Pinto Restaurant and Cantina, 10500 4th St. NW, Albuquerque; (505) 898-1771; www.elpinto.com

Frontier Restaurant, 2400 Central Ave. SE, Albuquerque; (505) 266-0550; www.frontierrestaurant.com

Taj Mahal, 1430 Carlisle Blvd. NE, Albuquerque; (505) 255-1994; www.tajmahalcuisineofindia.com

Corrales Bosque Trail

Located in northern Albuquerque, the Corrales Bosque Trail offers mountain bikers a great quick escape when you don't have time for a long drive. The trail offers beautiful views of the Rio Grande, provides many opportunities for birding, and even offers wildlife viewing.

Start: Rio Grande Valley State Park parking area, south of Alameda Boulevard and east of the Rio Grande.

Length: 13.0 miles out and back

Riding time: 2 to 3 hours

Best bike: Mountain bike

Terrain and trail surface: Paved trail at the beginning and then dirt and sand singletrack on a flat wooded trail along the Rio Grande

Traffic and hazards: Riders may encounter motorized vehicles along the paved section and hikers on the singletrack.

Map: USGS Los Griegos

Trail contacts: Open Space Division Parks and Recreation, 3615 Los Picaros Rd. SE, Albuquerque 87105; (505) 452-5200; www.cabq.gov/parksandrecreation/open-space

Special considerations: Rattlesnakes may be present along the trail.

Getting there: From I-25 in Albuquerque, take exit 233. Turn left (west) onto Atrisco Alameda Boulevard NE/NM 528 and drive 3.4 miles to the Rio Grande Valley State Park parking area, on the left. **GPS:** N35 11.678' / W106 38.375'

THE RIDE

Rio Grande State Park, located just minutes from downtown Albuquerque, is right on the central Rio Grande flyway. Park visitors can expect to see some of the 250 species of birds that live in or migrate through the area. The bosque, a riverside forest, has plenty of cottonwood trees to offer shade to riders and provides opportunities to see sandhill cranes, porcupines, roadrunners, and other wildlife.

Sandy portion of trail along the Rio Grande

The Corrales Bosque offers riders and nature lovers just what they'd expect from a bosque. It abounds with large cottonwood trees, and riders can weave through the bosque while catching glimpses of the Sandia Mountains that tower above Albuquerque to the east and even stop along the Rio Grande to enjoy some of the amazing wildlife that thrive in the area.

Pick up the easy-to-find Paseo del Bosque Recreation Trail at the northwest corner of the large and popular parking area. Turn right (north) onto the trail and ride just a short distance before turning left (northwest) at 0.1 mile to cross a small bridge over the drainage and then cross a large bridge over the Rio Grande. After crossing the large bridge, turn right (north) at 0.3 mile to ride on top of the levee for a short distance and then turn right (northeast) again to ride down off the levee onto the dirt trail below. There are a few trails here, but they all lead to the same place. No need to worry; a large levee acts as a handrail on the left (west) and the Rio Grande is on your right (east). Don't ride over the levee or into the water!

Continue riding northeast through the bosque as the trail winds and weaves. Here you will encounter a few places like the one mentioned at 1.5 miles where you can turn left (northwest) and ride up the levee. Continue straight across the road, not riding up the levee, to continue on the trail. There are also several meadows, including the one you encounter at 3.4 miles. These large openings are great places to slow down and watch closely for some of the area's wildlife. Be on the lookout for foxes, coyotes, and roadrunners.

At 5.2 miles the trail tightly hugs the levee on the left (west) and then turns right (east), back into a thickly wooded section of the bosque. Not long after, the thick section the forest thins a bit; there was a fire in this area a few years back. The trail eventually pops out along the Rio Grande for a short stretch at 6.4 miles before arriving at a large ramp at 6.5 miles. You can ride up the ramp and return to the trailhead parking area via the levee or return via the same for a round-trip of 13.0 miles.

MILES AND DIRECTIONS

0.0 Start on the paved Paseo del Bosque Recreation Trail and turn right (north).

0.1 Turn left (northwest) to cross a small bridge over the drainage and then a large bridge over the Rio Grande.

0.3 Turn right (north) onto the levee after crossing the large bridge.

0.4 Turn right (northeast) down off the levee onto the unsigned dirt trail.

1.5 Continue straight across the service road.

3.4 Ride through a large opening.

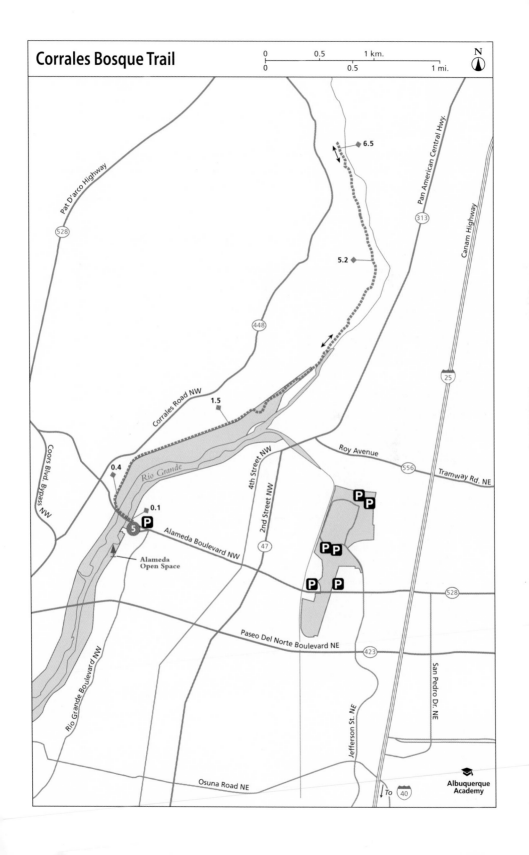

5.2   The trail tightly hugs the levee on the left (west).

6.4   Ride along the Rio Grande.

6.5   Turn left (west) up the ramp to return via the levee, or turn around and return via the trail.

13.0   Arrive back at the trailhead parking area.

RIDE INFORMATION

Local Attractions/Events
Balloon Fiesta Park, 5000 Balloon Fiesta Pkwy. NE, Albuquerque; (505) 821-1000; www.balloonfiesta.com

Petroglyph National Monument Visitor Center, 6001 Unser Blvd. NW, Albuquerque; (505) 899-0205; www.nps.gov/petr/index.htm

Local Bike Shops
Bikeworks Albuquerque, 2839 Carlisle Blvd. NE, Albuquerque; (505) 884-0341; www.bikeworksabq.com

Cycle Cave, Inc., 5716 Menaul Blvd. NE, Albuquerque; (505) 884-6607

Fat Tire Cycles, 421 Montaño Rd. NE, Albuquerque; (505) 345-9005; www.fattirecycles.com

Performance Bicycle Shop, 1431 Mercantile Ave. NE, Albuquerque; (505) 765-2471; www.performancebike.com

REI, 1550 Mercantile Ave., Albuquerque; (505) 247-1191; www.REI.com

Sport Systems, 6915 Montgomery Blvd. NE, Albuquerque; (505) 837-9400; www.nmsportsystems.com

Restaurants
El Patio De Albuquerque, 142 Harvard Dr. SE, Albuquerque; (505) 268-4245; www.elpatiodealbuquerque.com

Monroe's, 6051 Osuna Rd. NE, Albuquerque; (505) 881-4224; www.monroeschile.com

Range Café, 4401 Wyoming Blvd. NE, Albuquerque; (505) 293-2633; www.rangecafe.com

North Diversion Channel Trail

Albuquerque has been voted one of the top ten bike-friendly cities in the United States for good reason. Trails like the North Diversion Channel run through the city and help connect residents from one side of town to the other. University of New Mexico students frequent the southern portion of this trail, as it runs directly into campus.

Start: Northwest corner of the Balloon Fiesta Museum parking lot

Length: 15.4 miles out and back

Riding time: 2 to 4 hours

Best bike: Hybrid

Terrain and trail surface: Paved trail; gentle downhill for the ride out and slight uphill for the return ride

Traffic and hazards: Motorized vehicles are not permitted on the trail except for emergency and service vehicles. Riders may encounter walkers and runners.

Maps: USGS Los Griegos; detailed trail maps available at most area bike shops

Trail contacts: Open Space Division Parks and Recreation, 3615 Los Picaros Rd. SE, Albuquerque 87105; (505) 452-5200; www.cabq.gov/parksandrecreation/open-space

Special considerations: Be prepared to pack out trash from picnic areas, and respect private property along the trail.

Getting there: From I-25 in Albuquerque, take exit 233 and turn left (west) onto Alameda Boulevard. Drive 1 mile on Alameda Boulevard and then turn right (north) onto Balloon Museum Drive NE. Continue 0.8 mile to the parking area. **GPS:** N35 19.154' / W106 59.842'

THE RIDE

Begin your ride from the Balloon Fiesta Museum parking area. Most days of the year this large parking space sits empty and can even appear deserted. However, for nine days in October this area hosts the city's largest tourist draw. Every hotel in Albuquerque and the surrounding area can fill up for the Balloon Fiesta that fills the sky with hundreds of hot air balloons.

Trail along the North Diversion Channel

The North Diversion Channel that runs north–south through the city was designed to carry floodwaters from the channel and its tributaries to the Rio Grande. Because the desert is so dry, heavy rains here tend to run right across the ground rather than be absorbed. Flash floods occur quite regularly during heavy rains, and the North Diversion and other channels help protect the city and its residents.

From the northwest corner of the parking area, begin riding northwest on the paved North Diversion Channel Trail. Cross a bridge over the channel at 0.3 mile and then turn left (south) to ride south along the channel. Unlike most rides in this guide, the North Diversion Channel Trail offers access to more industrial parts of the city. Cross under Alameda Boulevard at 0.9 mile and under Paseo Del Norte at 1.6 miles. Not too far past Paseo Del Norte, you come to the Journal Center Access at 2.1 miles. This access leads to the offices of the *Albuquerque Journal*, New Mexico's largest newspaper.

Continue south past the Journal Center Access as the trail continues to go under major road crossings through the city. At 2.8 miles stay left to go under Osuna Road; turn left at 3.2 miles to cross the channel and then right to continue south. At 3.7 miles you reach one of only two road crossings on the trail. After crossing, continue to 4.2 miles, where you turn right (west) to cross a bridge and then left (south) to go under I-25. You'll ride under Montgomery Boulevard at 4.7 miles and then pass Paseo del Nordeste Recreation Trail at 5.0 miles on your left (east). Ride under three more roads after this point—Comanche Road at 5.3 miles, Candelaria Road at 5.8 miles, and Menaul Boulevard at 6.3 miles.

At 6.4 miles stay left at a fork to ride under I-40. If you go right at the fork you will ride onto the I-40 Trail. After going under I-40 the trail curves to the right (west) and travels along I-40 for a short stretch before turning south again and then crossing over Indian School Road at 7.3 miles. Reach the University of New Mexico campus at 7.7 miles. Turn around and return to the trailhead parking area via the same route for a round-trip of 15.4 miles.

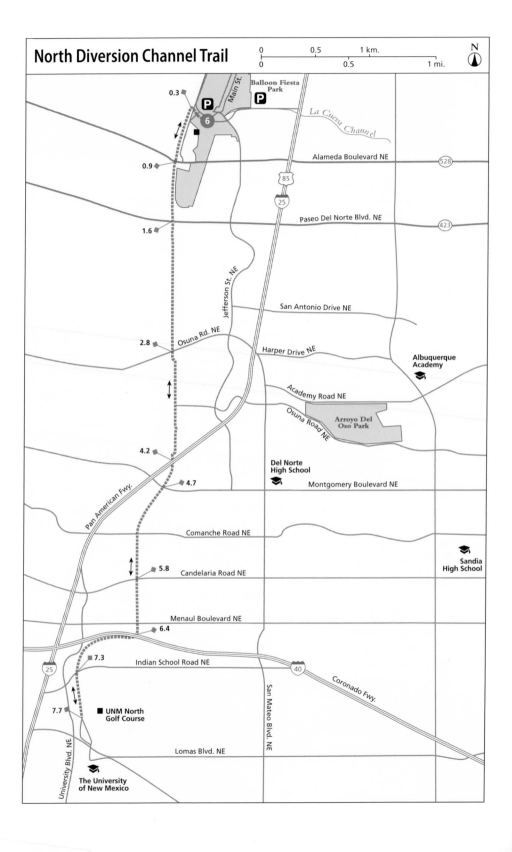

MILES AND DIRECTIONS

0.0 Start on the paved North Diversion Channel Trail and begin riding northwest.

0.3 Cross the bridge over the channel and turn left (south).

0.9 The trail travels under Alameda Boulevard.

1.6 Ride under Paseo Del Norte.

2.1 Left (east) is Journal Center Access. Continue riding south.

2.8 Stay left to go under Osuna Road. (Staying right will cause you to cross the main road.)

3.2 The trail turns left (east) to go over the channel and then turns right (south) to continue.

3.7 Cross a road.

4.2 Turn right (west) to ride over the bridge across the channel and then turn left (south) to ride under I-25.

4.7 Ride under Montgomery Boulevard.

5.0 Pass Paseo del Nordeste Recreation Trail on the left (east).

5.3 Ride under Comanche Road.

5.8 Ride under Candelaria Road.

6.3 Ride under Menaul Boulevard.

6.4 Stay left to ride under I-40. (Right leads to the I-40 Trail.)

7.3 Cross over Indian School Road.

7.7 Arrive at the University of New Mexico Campus. Return the way you came.

15.4 Arrive back at the trailhead parking area.

RIDE INFORMATION

Local Attractions/Events
Balloon Fiesta Park, 5000 Balloon Fiesta Pkwy. NE, Albuquerque; (505) 821-1000; www.balloonfiesta.com
Petroglyph National Monument Visitor Center, 6001 Unser Blvd. NW, Albuquerque 87120; (505) 899-0205; www.nps.gov/petr/index.htm

Local Bike Shops
The Bike Coop, 120 Yale Blvd. SE, Albuquerque; (505) 265-5170; www.bikecoop.com

The Bike Smith, 901 Rio Grande Blvd. NW, Albuquerque; (505) 242-9253; www.thebikesmith.com

Routes, Rentals, and Tours, 404 San Filipe St. NW, Albuquerque; (505) 933-5667; http://routesrentals.com

Trek Bicycle Superstore, 5000 Menaul Blvd. NE, Albuquerque; (505) 312-7243; www.trekbicyclesuperstore.com

Two Wheel Drive, 1706 Central Ave. SE, Albuquerque; (505) 243-8443; www .twowheeldrive.com

Restaurants

El Pinto Restaurant and Cantina, 10500 4th St. NW, Albuquerque; (505) 898-1771; www.elpinto.com

Frontier Restaurant, 2400 Central Ave. SE, Albuquerque; (505) 266-0550; www.frontierrestaurant.com

Taj Mahal, 1430 Carlisle Blvd. NE, Albuquerque; (505) 255-1994; www.taj mahalcuisineofindia.com

Paseo del Nordeste Recreation Trail

The Paseo del Nordeste Recreation Trail is another of Albuquerque's trails that takes advantage of the space used by a diversion channel. The trail follows a large concrete channel and passes several small public use areas and through several small neighborhoods.

Start: Trailhead on the west side of Pennsylvania Street, directly across from the Sandia High School trailhead parking area

Length: 6.2 miles out and back

Riding time: 1 to 2 hours

Best bike: Hybrid

Terrain and trail surface: Flat paved trail

Traffic and hazards: Motorized vehicles are not permitted on the trail. Riders may encounter walkers and runners.

Maps: USGS Los Griegos; detailed trail maps available at most area bike shops

Trail contacts: Open Space Division Parks and Recreation, 3615 Los Picaros Rd. SE, Albuquerque 87105; (505) 452-5200; www.cabq.gov/parksandrecreation/open-space

Special considerations: Be prepared to pack out trash from picnic areas, and respect private property along the trail.

Getting there: From Albuquerque, take I-40 East to exit 161; turn left (north) onto San Mateo Boulevard. Drive 1.2 miles north on San Mateo Boulevard and turn right (east) onto Candelaria Road. Continue 1.5 miles and turn left (north) onto Pennsylvania Street. Drive 0.2 mile to the Sandia High School trailhead parking area on the right (east). **GPS:** N35 11.897' / W106 55.975'

THE RIDE

The Paseo del Nordeste Recreation Trail traverses a series of northeastern neighborhoods in Albuquerque as it travels along the Hahn Arroyo. The trail runs west and east, so the ride out will be slightly downhill as you travel away from the mountains and the return will have a gradual ascent as you head back toward the Sandias.

From the trailhead, begin riding west on the paved trail. A sign for the trail hangs just above the access. Parking at Sandia High School is permitted for trail users. There are numerous road crossings on this trail, the first at 0.6 mile where you cross Louisiana Boulevard. Many of the crossings are not super busy, but a couple have a good bit of traffic. Cross over California Street at 1.0 mile and continue riding as the trail turns northwest and then crosses San Pedro Drive at 1.2 miles.

At 1.5 miles you cross Comanche Road and then ride past Montgomery Park on the right (north). The park is very busy on nice days and sees a lot of

Resting point along the Paseo del Nordeste Trail

Paseo del Nordeste Recreation Trail

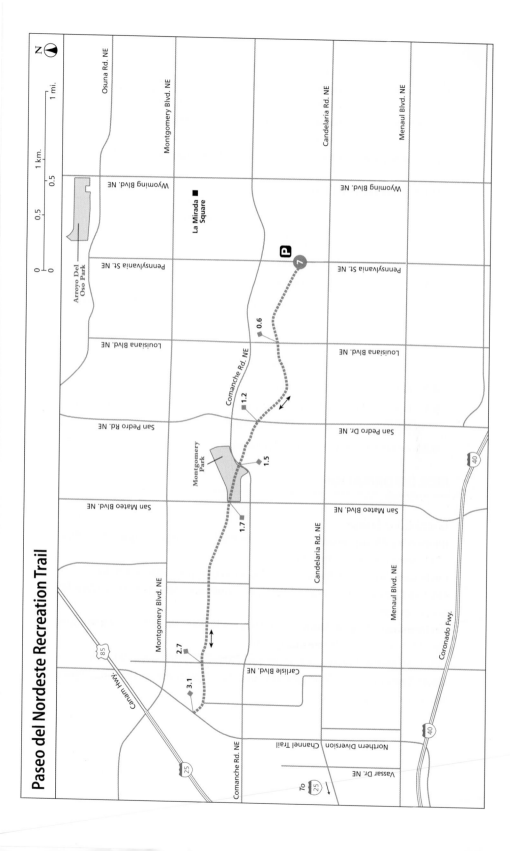

North Foothills Trail

The North Foothills Trail offers mountain bikers a great opportunity to ride rolling singletrack almost any day of the year. This fun 11.6-mile out-and-back trail provides great access to several other trails—allowing riders to customize their route in both distance and technicality!

Start: Sandia Peak Tramway parking area

Length: 11.6 miles out and back

Riding time: 2 to 4 hours

Best bike: Mountain bike

Terrain and trail surface: Smooth singletrack, some technical rocky areas, rolling hills, several moderate climbs

Traffic and hazards: One road crossing; rattlesnake, black bear, and mountain lion sightings are possible.

Maps: USGS Sandia Crest; trail map available at the Sandia Ranger District visitor center

Trail contacts: Cibola National Forest—Sandia Ranger District, 11776 Hwy. 337, Tijeras 87059; (505) 281-3304; www.fs.usda.gov/main/cibola/home

Special considerations: Ride early or late in the summer months, and carry plenty of water.

Getting there: From Albuquerque, take I-25 North to exit 234 toward NM 556/Tramway Road. Turn right (east) onto NM 556/Tramway Road. After 4.9 miles turn left (east) to stay on Tramway Road NE. Drive 1 mile to the tramway fee station; pay the parking fee and continue 0.1 mile to the parking area. **GPS:** N35 11.487' / W106 28.759'

THE RIDE

The Foothills Trail is also known as and marked Trail #365. It certainly seems plausible that it is called Trail #365 because one could easily use this trail 365 days a year! With something like 300 days of sunshine per year, Albuquerque is a pretty ideal place to ride.

Part of the trail system known as the Sandia Mountain Trails, the Foothills Trail is located in the Sandia Ranger District of the Cibola National Forest. The trail follows the western slope of the Sandia Mountains and roughly parallels the boundary of the Sandia Mountain Wilderness. *Note:* Bikes are not allowed in the wilderness.

Due to its proximity to Albuquerque, several good access points, and the fact that it is overall an amazing trail, the Foothills Trail sees its fair share of traffic. It's popular with hikers, trail runners, and mountain bikers, so be on the lookout for other users, particularly on rolling hills and sharp corners. Although trail etiquette requires bikers to yield to hikers, you will find that most hikers and runners on this trail will happily step to the side to allow bikers to pass. "Excuse me" and "Thank you" go a long way toward keeping the peace on multiuse trails, so be sure to use both phrases liberally! The trail features a good amount of fast and curvy singletrack, with a few portions of rocky, technical riding. It is a good choice for beginner to intermediate mountain bikers.

From the southeast corner of the Sandia Peak Tramway parking area, begin riding on the obvious dirt/rock path. The trail immediately begins a moderate to steep ascent to the southeast as it climbs toward the water tower.

At 0.2 mile come to a fork in the trail. Stay right (south) to stay on the Foothills Trail. A sign here points you toward the "Elena Gallegos Trail"; this is actually the Foothills Trail/Trail 365 and leads to the Elena Gallegos Open Space, also called the Elena Gallegos Picnic Area and Albert G. Simms Park. The 640-acre Elena Gallegos Open Space offers a picnic area and access to several trails. The trail to the left (west) provides access to the Sandia Mountain Wilderness—remember, bikes are not allowed in wilderness areas.

Come to another fork in the trail at 0.4 mile. Stay south (right); the trail to the east (left) leads into the Sandia Mountain Wilderness.

At 0.7 mile you come to the first technical portion of the trail. Loose gravel and some larger rocks will require some careful maneuvering. If you can manage this portion of the trail, you'll easily be able to ride the rest of the trail. Come to another trail intersection at 1.0 mile. Continue south; the cross trail (heading east and west) provides access to the Sandia Mountain Wilderness.

At 1.8 miles come to the intersection with Trail #230, also known as the Domingo Baca Trail. Stay right (south) to continue on the Foothills Trail/Trail

Cane cholla along the Foothills Trail

#365. Come to a fencerow at 2.6 miles. The trail turns sharply to the right (west). Get ready to have some fun—this portion of the trail is smooth, fast, and mostly downhill!

Reach another intersection with Trail #230/Domingo Baca Trail. Again, stay south to continue on the Foothills Trail/Trail #365. Cross Simms Park Road at 3.2 miles and continue south. This road leads east to the Elena Gallegos Open Space, which provides access to several other trails for riders who want to lengthen this ride. A decent map is available at the information center, located at the east end of Simms Park Road.

At 4.0 miles you come to the intersection with Trails #305 and #366, both of which are trails in the Elena Gallegos Open Space. Stay right (south) to continue on the Foothills Trail.

Cross an unmarked gravel road at 4.2 miles and continue south. At 4.6 miles come to a trail intersection; stay left (south). The trail to the right (west) leads to Bear Canyon Arroyo. After a very short distance come to Trail #305; continue south on the Foothills Trail/Trail #365. At 4.8 miles you reach the intersection with the Michial M. Emery Bear Canyon Trail; continue south. The trail becomes rocky and more technical once again as you skirt the eastern boundary of a subdivision just before it terminates at the Foothills Trail System parking area at 5.8 miles. Turn around and return to the tramway and trailhead via the same route for a round-trip of 11.6 miles.

Option: Navigate a few of the neighborhood streets and access the South Foothills Trail, also signed "Trail #365."

MILES AND DIRECTIONS

0.0 Start from the southeast corner of the Sandia Peak Tramway parking area and begin riding on the obvious dirt/rock path.

0.2 Come to a fork in the trail. Stay right (south) to stay on the Foothills Trail.

0.4 Stay south (right). The trail to the east (left) leads into the Sandia Mountain Wilderness.

0.7 Come to the first technical portion of the trail.

1.0 Continue south. The cross trail (heading east and west) provides access to the Sandia Mountain Wilderness.

1.8 Reach the intersection with Trail #230, also known as the Domingo Baca Trail. Stay right (south) to continue on the Foothills Trail/Trail #365.

3.2 Cross Simms Park Road.

4.0 Come to the trail intersection with Trails #305 and #366, both of which are trails in the Elena Gallegos Open Space. Stay right (south) to continue on the Foothills Trail.

4.2 Cross an unmarked gravel road.

4.6 Come to a trail intersection; stay left (south). The trail to the right (west) leads to Bear Canyon Arroyo.

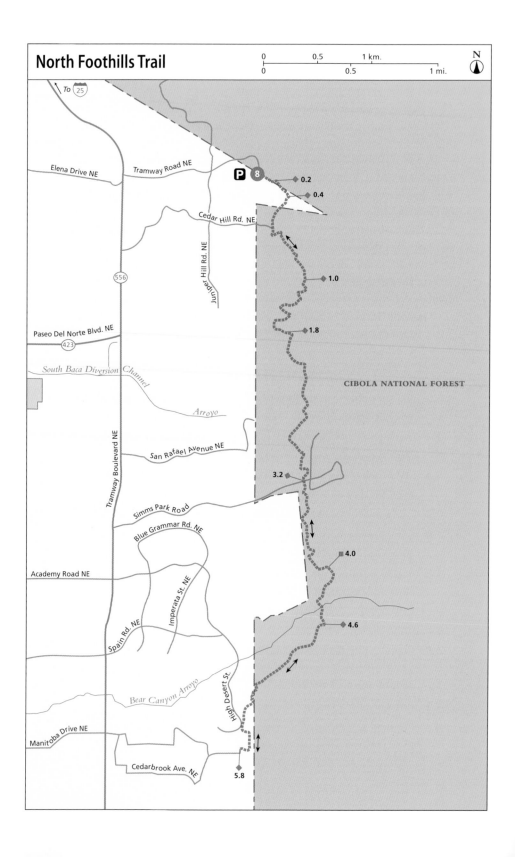

North Foothills Trail

0   0.5   1 km.

0   0.5   1 mi.

N

To 25

Elena Drive NE   Tramway Road NE

P 8   0.2

0.4

Cedar Hill Rd. NE

Juniper Hill Rd. NE

556

Paseo Del Norte Blvd. NE

423

South Baca Diversion Channel

Arroyo

San Rafael Avenue NE

Tramway Boulevard NE

3.2

Simms Park Road

Blue Grammar Rd. NE

Academy Road NE

Imperata St. NE

Spain Rd. NE

Bear Canyon Arroyo

High Desert St.

Manitoba Drive NE

Cedarbrook Ave. NE

5.8

1.0

1.8

CIBOLA NATIONAL FOREST

4.0

4.6

4.8 Reach the intersection with the Michial M. Emery Bear Canyon Trail; continue south.

5.8 Reach the Foothills Trail System parking area. Return the way you came.

11.6 Arrive back at the trailhead parking area.

RIDE INFORMATION

Local Attraction

Sandia Peak Ski and Tramway, 30 Tramway Rd. NE, Albuquerque; (505) 856-7325; http://sandiapeak.com

Local Bike Shops

The Bike Coop, 120 Yale Blvd. SE, Albuquerque; (505) 265-5170; www.bike coop.com

The Bike Smith, 901 Rio Grande Blvd. NW, Albuquerque; (505) 242-9253; www.thebikesmith.com

Routes, Rentals, and Tours, 404 San Filipe St. NW, Albuquerque; (505) 933-5667; www.routesrentals.com

Trek Bicycle Superstore, 5000 Menaul Blvd. NE, Albuquerque; (505) 312-7243; www.trekbicyclesuperstore.com

Two Wheel Drive, 1706 Central Ave. SE, Albuquerque; (505) 243-8443; www .twowheeldrive.com

Restaurants

El Pinto Restaurant and Cantina, 10500 4th St. NW, Albuquerque; (505) 898-1771; www.elpinto.com

Frontier Restaurant, 2400 Central Ave. SE, Albuquerque; (505) 266-0550; www.frontierrestaurant.com

Taj Mahal, 1430 Carlisle Blvd. NE, Albuquerque; (505) 255-1994; www.taj mahalcuisineofindia.com

South Foothills Trail

The Foothills Trail (#365) is one of the more popular trails in the Sandia Mountains because it is so easily accessed from the city limits. This section is located near the Embudo Trail, and many riders use it. Because of its lower elevation, it is a great choice for a winter ride, when many of the other trails in the Sandia Mountains are icy or snow packed.

Start: Trailhead at southern end of the parking lot

Length: 4.9-mile loop

Riding time: 1 to 2 hours

Best bike: Mountain bike

Terrain and trail surface: Packed-dirt singletrack filled with ups and downs and a few exposed sections

Traffic and hazards: Motorized vehicles are not permitted on the trail. Riders may encounter hikers and equestrians.

Maps: USGS Sandia Crest; trail map available at the Sandia Ranger District visitor center

Trail contacts: Cibola National Forest—Sandia Ranger District, 11776 Hwy. 337, Tijeras 87059; (505) 281-3304; www.fs.usda.gov/main/cibola/home

Special considerations: Ride early or late in the summer months, and carry plenty of water.

Getting there: From Albuquerque, take I-40 east to exit 167 toward Tramway Boulevard/NM556. Turn left (north) onto Tramway Boulevard. Drive 2.1 miles and turn right (east) onto Indian School Road. Continue 1.1 miles to the parking area trailhead. **GPS:** N35 09.907' / W106 47.994'

THE RIDE

Many describe the Sandia Mountains as being in Albuquerque's backyard. This trail takes that statement literally, as it balances on the fine line between an urban trail and a wilderness trail. There are several spots near the beginning of the ride where the trail scoots around a small neighborhood, and it may be hard to believe that you are actually in the Sandia Mountain Wilderness Area.

Trail 401 forms the western portion of this loop trail.

As the South Foothills Trail begins to gain elevation, it gains a more wilderness feel, and it may be hard to believe that civilization is so close. This is particularly true in winter, when the trail sees less use.

The trailhead for Trail 401 is located just south of the parking area, next to the informational kiosk. Several unmarked and undesignated trails break off from the trail and head west toward the neighborhood below the trail. Ignore these as the trail runs south along the base of the Sandia Mountains. This is a great trail during cooler months, as it's fairly easy to navigate, even in snow. The lack of shade on the trail makes it less desirable during summer.

Turn right (west) at the kiosk to ride uphill on Trail #401, and quickly keep right to stay on Trail #401. Left is Trail #365A, your return trail. After a short climb the trail heads downhill and crosses an area where numerous "undesignated" trails intersect the main trail. Continue south on the obvious main trail and continue to watch for land manager signs indicating that you are on Trail #401. At 1.4 miles the trail does a tricky zigzag but is signed well; the first sign points left (east) and the second points right (south). At 1.5 miles you ride past the South Lomas Channel and then reach an access trail to the Copper Trailhead at 1.6 miles. Stay left (south) on Trail #401, crossing Trail #400 at 1.7 miles.

After a short uphill you will pass the Hilldale Loop Trail on the right (east) at 2.1 miles and then stay left (southeast) onto Trail #375 for a short distance before turning left (northeast) again onto Trail #365, the Foothills Trail. Continue on Trail 365 as it turns north and slowly climbs higher and higher into the foothills. You'll cross over Trail 400 again at 2.7 miles and continue riding north. Continue uphill as the trail switchbacks a few times and then reaches a saddle at 3.0 miles. U Mound is to the left (northwest); stay right (east) to head downhill and then up again.

Cross a small footbridge at 4.1 miles just before reaching a second saddle, and then make two quick lefts at 4.3 miles onto Trail 365A. Cross a second bridge at 4.5 miles and continue along the rocky trail as it slowly descends and reconnects with Trail 401. Turn right (northeast) to return to the trailhead parking area at 4.9 miles.

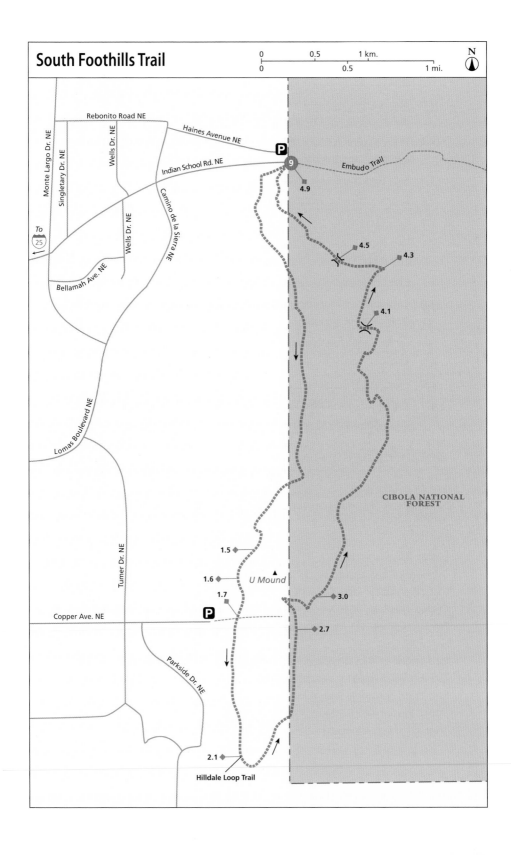

South Foothills Trail

0   0.5   1 km.

0   0.5   1 mi.

N

Rebonito Road NE

Monte Largo Dr. NE

Singletary Dr. NE

Wells Dr. NE

Haines Avenue NE

Indian School Rd. NE

Embudo Trail

To 25

Wells Dr. NE

Camino de la Sierra NE

Bellamah Ave. NE

9

4.9

4.5

4.3

4.1

Lomas Boulevard NE

CIBOLA NATIONAL
FOREST

Turner Dr. NE

1.5

1.6

U Mound

1.7

3.0

Copper Ave. NE

2.7

Parkside Dr. NE

2.1

Hilldale Loop Trail

MILES AND DIRECTIONS

0.0 Start at the kiosk and turn right (west) to ride uphill on Trail 401; quickly keep right to stay on Trail 401.

1.4 The trail does a tricky zigzag but is signed well; the first sign points left (east) and the second points right (south).

1.5 Ride past the South Lomas Channel.

1.6 Reach an access trail to the Copper Trailhead. Stay straight (south).

1.7 Cross Trail 400.

2.1 Pass the Hilldale Loop Trail on the right (east). Stay left onto Trail 375 and then Trail 365.

2.7 Cross over Trail 400.

3.0 Continue uphill as the trail switchbacks a few times and then reaches a saddle near U Mound.

4.1 Cross a small footbridge.

4.3 Make two left turns onto Trail 365A and then ride west on Trail 365A.

4.5 Cross a second footbridge.

4.9 Turn right (northeast) to reconnect with Trail 401 and arrive back at the trailhead parking area.

RIDE INFORMATION

Local Attraction
Sandia Peak Ski and Tramway, 30 Tramway Rd. NE, Albuquerque; (505) 856-7325; http://sandiapeak.com

Local Bike Shops
Bikeworks Albuquerque, 2839 Carlisle Blvd. NE, Albuquerque; (505) 884-0341; www.bikeworksabq.com
Cycle Cave, Inc., 5716 Menaul Blvd. NE, Albuquerque; (505) 884-6607
Fat Tire Cycles, 421 Montaño Rd. NE, Albuquerque; (505) 345-9005; www.fat tirecycles.com
Performance Bicycle Shop, 1431 Mercantile Ave. NE, Albuquerque; (505) 765-2471; www.performancebike.com
REI, 1550 Mercantile Ave., Albuquerque; (505) 247-1191; www.REI.com
Sport Systems, 6915 Montgomery Blvd. NE, Albuquerque; (505) 837-9400; www.nmsportsystems.com

Restaurants

El Patio De Albuquerque, 142 Harvard Dr. SE, Albuquerque; (505) 268-4245; www.elpatiodealbuquerque.com

Monroe's, 6051 Osuna Rd. NE, Albuquerque; (505) 881-4224; www.monroes chile.com

Range Café, 4401 Wyoming Blvd. NE, Albuquerque; (505) 293-2633; www .rangecafe.com

Tijeras Trot

The Tijeras Trot, as locals call it, is a very popular road bike ride that can be used as a warm-up for riders looking to extend their ride on either NM 337, which goes south from Tijeras, or on NM 14, which goes north from Tijeras. Both extended rides offer great views and a good workout.

Start: Four Hills Village Shopping Center parking area

Length: 13.8 miles out and back

Riding time: 2 to 3 hours

Best bike: Road bike

Terrain and trail surface: Road ride with a wide shoulder on both sides; gradual uphill on the out portion and then downhill on the return

Traffic and hazards: Motorized vehicles are present, as this is a road ride; however, most traffic tends to use I-40.

Map: USGS Sandia Crest

Trail contacts: Cibola National Forest—Sandia Ranger District, 11776 Hwy. 337, Tijeras 87059; (505) 281-3304; www.fs.usda.gov/main/cibola/home

Special considerations: Be careful and watch for cars when riding on roads. Watch for debris, glass, and trash on the shoulders.

Getting there: From Albuquerque, take I-40 East to exit 167 and turn right (south) onto Tramway Boulevard/NM 556. Drive 0.1 mile and park at the Four Hills Village Shopping Center, on the right (west). **GPS:** N35 06.772' / W106 49.830'

THE RIDE

The village of Tijeras is a very old community and quite rich in culture. When the San Antonio and Tijeras Pueblos, located near the USDA Forest Service Sandia Ranger Station on NM 337, were excavated, they showed evidence that human land use in the area dated back to as late as the 1200s! Tijeras is a small village with just around 500 residents, but it's a great starting point to outdoor adventure in the nearby forests and mountains. Nestled at the base of the Sandia Mountains, Tijeras offers access points to great mountain biking just to the south in the Manzano Mountains and amazing hiking opportunities and even more mountain biking to the north in the Sandia Mountains. Road bikers also thrive here. They can access the winding roads of the Sandia Mountains and the Sandia Crest Road as well as the scenic beauty of the Turquoise Trail National Scenic Byway, which runs from Tijeras to Santa Fe.

The Tijeras Trot is a great ride up the Tijeras Canyon, and history lovers take note: It follows Historic Route 66! The climb on the ride is quite moderate,

Wide shoulder along Tijeras Trot

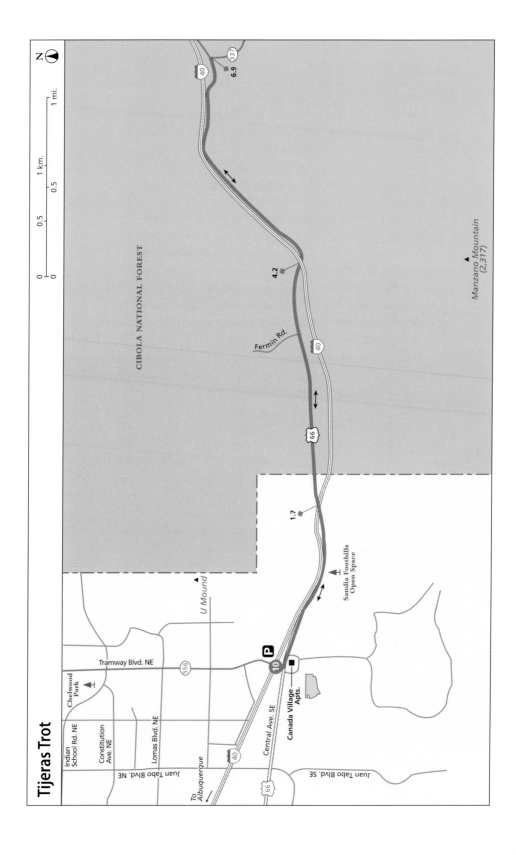

Tijeras Trot

and the shoulders on either side of the road are in pretty good condition as well as being spacious. On nice days you can expect to see plenty of other cyclists on the road, as the heavier motorized traffic tends to use I-40, which runs parallel to this route.

Leave the Four Hills Village Shopping Center and begin riding southeast along the famous Historic Route 66. Traffic will be a bit heavier here until you leave the busy square and cross over 4 Hills Road at 0.2 mile, where cars can access I-40. Continue riding southeast as traffic gets lighter and you leave the hustle and bustle of the city behind. You will pass the Sandia Foothills Open Space area on the right (south) just as the road turns due east and then crosses over I-40 at 1.7 miles. Watch for a little extra traffic here as cars try navigating on and off I-40. From here you can cruise a bit as the road passes several quiet neighborhoods in the southern Sandia Mountains.

At 4.2 miles the road passes under I-40 and then turns northeast as you begin to climb a little bit. The trees and mountains through this section offer spectacular views, especially in fall. The road eventually turns due east again. You arrive at the Tijeras city limits at 6.5 miles and then the lone stoplight at 6.9 miles. Riders looking to extend can turn right (south) to take on the winding roads of NM 337 or can continue straight (northeast) to access NM 14 and the Turquoise Trail National Scenic Byway. For this description, turn around here and return to the Four Hills Village Shopping Center and parking area for a round-trip of 13.8 miles.

MILES AND DIRECTIONS

0.0 Start from the Four Hills Village Shopping Center and begin riding southeast along Historic Route 66.

0.2 Continue southeast across 4 Hills Road SE.

1.7 Route 66 passes over I-40.

4.2 Route 66 passes under I-40.

6.5 Pass the Tijeras city limit sign.

6.9 Arrive at the stoplight in the middle of Tijeras. Return the way you came.

13.8 Arrive back at the shopping center parking lot.

RIDE INFORMATION

Local Attraction
National Museum of Nuclear Science & History, 601 Eubank Blvd. SE, Albuquerque; (505) 245-2137; www.nuclearmuseum.org

Local Bike Shops

The Bike Coop, 120 Yale Blvd. SE, Albuquerque; (505) 265-5170; www.bike coop.com

The Bike Smith, 901 Rio Grande Blvd. NW, Albuquerque; (505) 242-9253; www.thebikesmith.com

Routes, Rentals, and Tours, 404 San Filipe St. NW, Albuquerque; (505) 933-5667; http://routesrentals.com

Trek Bicycle Superstore, 5000 Menaul Blvd. NE, Albuquerque; (505) 312-7243; www.trekbicyclesuperstore.com

Two Wheel Drive, 1706 Central Ave. SE, Albuquerque; (505) 243-8443; www .twowheeldrive.com

Restaurants

El Pinto Restaurant and Cantina, 10500 4th St. NW, Albuquerque; (505) 898-1771; www.elpinto.com

Frontier Restaurant, 2400 Central Ave. SE, Albuquerque; (505) 266-0550; www.frontierrestaurant.com

Taj Mahal, 1430 Carlisle Blvd. NE, Albuquerque; (505) 255-1994; www.taj mahalcuisineofindia.com

East of Albuquerque

Tree Spring Trail (Ride 15)

Most people don't think of mountains when they think of New Mexico, but just east of Albuquerque, the prominent Sandia Mountains stand at an elevation of over 10,000 feet. Recreational opportunities abound in the Sandias—from skiing to hiking to biking. And that's not all. Just east of Albuquerque, the charming town of Tijeras offers visitors a gateway into the Cibola National Forest. Cibola offers archaeological sites and primitive canyons for exploring, and the mountain biking is great for those looking for a challenge.

Blue Ribbon, Gnasty, and Otero Canyon Trails Loop

This little ride connects three trails in the Cibola National Forest for a super fun loop. Start out with a somewhat steep and technical climb before hitting a flat ridgeline, a fun downhill, and then a fast section at the end through Otero Canyon.

Start: Otero Canyon trailhead parking area on the south side of NM 337

Length: 5.3-mile loop

Riding time: 1 to 2 hours

Best bike: Mountain bike

Terrain and trail surface: Dirt singletrack trail the entire route. The trail begins flat then climbs steeply out of the canyon before a downhill return to the Otero Canyon floor.

Traffic and hazards: No motorized vehicles are permitted on the trail. Riders may encounter hikers, trail runners, and equestrians.

Maps: USGS Sedillo; trail map available at the Sandia Ranger District visitor center

Trail contacts: Cibola National Forest—Sandia Ranger District, 11776 Hwy. 337, Tijeras 87059; (505) 281-3304; www.fs.usda.gov/main/cibola/home

Special considerations: The trail borders military property in some places; the military property is patrolled, so be sure to stay on the trail.

Getting there: From Albuquerque, take I-40 East for about 15 miles to exit 175 for NM 337/NM 333 toward Tijeras. Turn right (south) onto NM 337 and drive 3.9 miles to the Otero Canyon Trailhead parking area, on the right (south). **GPS:** N35 03.452' / W106 37.431'

THE RIDE

The Cibola National Forest in New Mexico comprises 1,633,783 acres of some of the most beautiful land the state has to offer. The national forest actually flows over into parts of west Texas and Oklahoma and includes Mount Taylor and the Bear, Datil, Galina, Magdalena, Manzano, Sandia, San Mateo, and Zuni Mountains through west and central New Mexico. Also included are four national grasslands. The most visited mountains in the forest, and in the state

Singletrack on the Blue Ribbon Trail

of New Mexico, are located here just east of Albuquerque, where you can find this ride.

The mountain bike trail system that has developed in the Manzano Mountains has been an ongoing project by the forest service and has become one of Albuquerque's fun quick getaways. Locals can reach these trails in a matter of minutes, depending on where they live in the city. Mountain bikers can easily fill up a weekend riding trails here and still have plenty more to ride for the next few weekends. The Blue Ribbon, Gnasty, and Otero Canyon loop makes for a fun and fast trip with a little something for every rider.

From the Otero Canyon Trailhead parking area on the south side NM 337, ride south on the paved road for just a brief distance before dropping down left (southeast) onto the packed dirt singletrack Otero Canyon Trail. The trail quickly levels out, and you pass the Cedro Creek Nature Trail, a foot-traffic-only trail, on the left (east) at 0.1 mile. Continue riding south until you arrive at a trail junction at 0.3 mile. Turn left at the junction onto the Blue Ribbon Trail. Right (west) is the Tunnel Canyon Trail. Straight (south) will be your return on the Otero Canyon Trail. After you turn left onto the Blue Ribbon Trail, the trail quickly begins climbing on a rugged and rocky surface. After a few switchbacks and a steep climb, you reach the end of the climb at 1.7 miles; the trail becomes much more flat and follows along a ridgeline.

Continue riding along the rocky trail as it circles around to the west of the highest point on the mountain and then passes through a large open meadow. Just after the meadow you arrive at a second trail junction. Turn right (west) onto the Gnasty Trail. The Blue Ribbon Trail continues left (southeast). Once you're on the Gnasty Trail, the trail tightens up a bit and prepares for a steep descent at 2.9 miles. After a fast, fun descent with a couple of sharp switchbacks, you arrive at Otero Canyon. Turn right (north) onto Otero Canyon Trail at 3.6 miles and begin your return. The canyon is a gradual descent that is mostly packed dirt but has a few rocky patches; it even includes a good jump at 4.5 miles.

Arrive at the final trail junction at 5.0 miles, the first trail junction you encountered. Stay straight (northwest) to return to the trailhead parking area. Right (north) is the Blue Ribbon Trail and left (west) is the Tunnel Canyon Trail. Return to the trailhead parking area at 5.3 miles.

MILES AND DIRECTIONS

0.0 Start from the trailhead and ride south on the paved road for just a brief distance before dropping down left (southeast) onto the packed dirt singletrack.

0.1 Pass the Cedro Creek Nature Trail on the left (east).

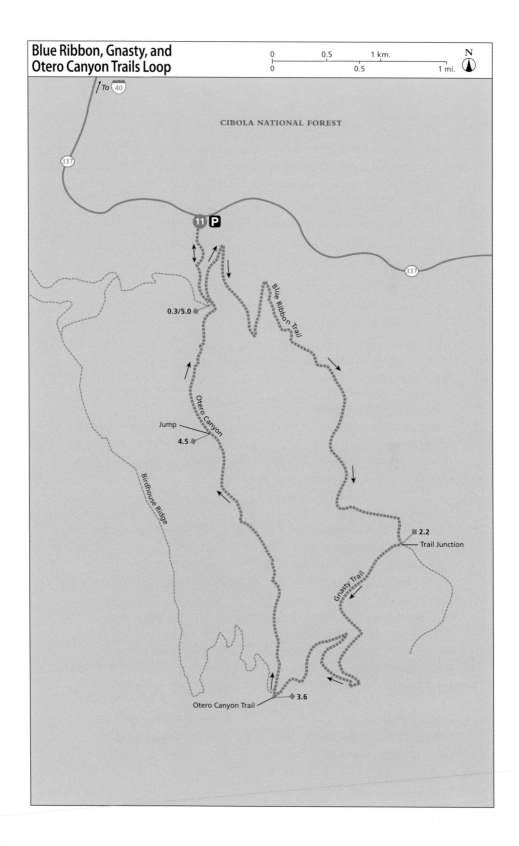

Blue Ribbon, Gnasty, and Otero Canyon Trails Loop

0   0.5   1 km.

0   0.5   1 mi.

N

To 40

CIBOLA NATIONAL FOREST

337

11 P

337

0.3/5.0

Blue Ribbon Trail

Otero Canyon

Jump

4.5

Birdhouse Ridge

2.2

Trail Junction

Gnasty Trail

Otero Canyon Trail

3.6

0.3 Arrive at a trail junction. Turn left (north) onto the Blue Ribbon Trail. Right (west) is the Tunnel Canyon Trail and straight (south) is your return trail.

1.7 Reach the end of steep climb and switchbacks.

2.2 Arrive at a second trail junction. Turn right (west) onto the Gnasty Trail. The Blue Ribbon Trail continues left (southeast).

2.9 Begin a steeper downhill section.

3.6 Turn right (north) onto the Otero Canyon Trail. Left (south) is a restricted area—do not enter.

3.7 Stay right (north) on the Otero Canyon Trail. Left (west) is the West Ridge Trail.

4.5 Enjoy the jump.

5.0 Arrive at the final trail junction. Stay straight (northwest) to return to the trailhead parking area.

5.3 Arrive back at the trailhead parking area.

RIDE INFORMATION

Local Attractions/Events

Tijeras Arts Market, 488 Hwy. 333, Tijeras; (505) 281-9611; www.tijerasartsmarket.com/toaam

Tijeras Pueblo Archaeological Site, 11776 Hwy. 337, Tijeras; http://friendsoftijeraspueblo.org/welcomehomepage.html

Local Bike Shops

Bikeworks Albuquerque, 2839 Carlisle Blvd. NE, Albuquerque; (505) 884-0341; www.bikeworksabq.com

Cycle Cave, Inc., 5716 Menaul Blvd. NE, Albuquerque; (505) 884-6607

Fat Tire Cycles, 421 Montaño Rd. NE, Albuquerque; (505) 345-9005; www.fattirecycles.com

Performance Bicycle Shop, 1431 Mercantile Ave. NE, Albuquerque; (505) 765-2471; www.performancebike.com

REI, 1550 Mercantile Ave., Albuquerque; (505) 247-1191; www.REI.com

Sport Systems, 6915 Montgomery Blvd. NE, Albuquerque; (505) 837-9400; www.nmsportsystems.com

Restaurants

El Patio De Albuquerque, 142 Harvard Dr. SE, Albuquerque; (505) 268-4245; www.elpatiodealbuquerque.com

Monroe's, 6051 Osuna Rd. NE, Albuquerque; (505) 881-4224; www.monroes chile.com

Range Café, 4401 Wyoming Blvd. NE, Albuquerque; (505) 293-2633; www .rangecafe.com

Tunnel Canyon Trail

The Tunnel Canyon Trail, shown on some maps as the Grand Enchantment Trail, is a well-known mountain biking trail to locals. Hikers and trail runners get just as much enjoyment out of the trail as mountain bikers do, especially due to the decent amount of shade provided along the trail. This 4.4-mile out-and-back ride will take you up the gradual ascent of Tunnel Canyon, over to Cedro Creek and Otero Canyon, and then back.

Start: Tunnel Canyon Trailhead parking area, on the west side of NM 337

Length: 4.4 miles out and back

Riding time: 1 to 2 hours

Best bike: Mountain bike

Terrain and trail surface: Dirt singletrack trail the entire route. The trail begins flat with a gradual ascent and then climbs steeply out of the canyon before a downhill to the Otero Canyon floor.

Traffic and hazards: No motorized vehicles are permitted on the trail. Riders may encounter hikers, trail runners, and equestrians.

Maps: USGS Sedillo; trail map available at Sandia Ranger District visitor center

Trail contacts: Cibola National Forest—Sandia Ranger District, 11776 Hwy. 337, Tijeras 87059; (505) 281-3304; www.fs.usda.gov/main/cibola/home

Special considerations: The trail borders military property in some places; be sure to stay on the trail.

Getting there: From Albuquerque, take I-40 East for about 15 miles to exit 175 for NM 337/NM 333 toward Tijeras. Turn right (south) onto NM 337 and drive 2.5 miles to the Tunnel Canyon Trailhead parking area, on the right (west) side of the road. **GPS:** N35 02.807' / W106 23.003'

THE RIDE

Tunnel Canyon is well known to locals as a mountain biking trail, but it's an excellent multiuse trail for most of the year because of its lower elevation for the winter months and the shade that trees provide for the summer months. The trail goes up through Tunnel Canyon and a beautiful pine forest. There is a military base to the west of the trail. The borders of the base are regularly patrolled, so do not cross over the boundary.

Cane cholla cactus on Tunnel Canyon Trail

Fleabane on Tunnel Canyon Trail

From the Tunnel Canyon Trailhead parking area, begin riding southwest through a meadow. After just 0.1 mile you reach a sign that reads "Tunnel Canyon Trail." Stay right and continue riding southwest through the remainder of the field as it begins to narrow and enter Tunnel Canyon. After 0.7 mile you come to a creek crossing that will more than likely be dry. Cross the creek and continue riding south as the trail begins to ascend slightly.

At 1.0 mile cross a small footbridge just before the trail makes a sharp left (northeast) turn and then a right (east) turn as the trail gradually climbs up and out of Tunnel Canyon. At 1.2 miles reach a rock outcropping on the left (north) that offers great views of the Sandia Mountains to the north. From this point the trail continues to climb and curves around an east-facing ridge just before the trail levels out and begins to descend at 1.8 miles.

Descend a short distance more before reaching the Otero Canyon floor and the junction with the Otero Canyon Trail at 2.2 miles. Turn around and return to the Tunnel Canyon Trailhead parking area via the same route for a round-trip of 4.4 miles.

MILES AND DIRECTIONS

0.0 Start from the Tunnel Canyon Trailhead parking area and head south on the unsigned trail.

0.1 Reach a Tunnel Canyon Trail sign. Stay right (southwest) on the Tunnel Canyon Trail and continue riding southwest.

0.7 Come to a creek crossing (probably dry) and continue riding south as the trail begins to climb a bit.

1.0 Cross a wooden footbridge just before the trail makes a sharp left (north) turn and then turns right (east). Begin riding out of Tunnel Canyon.

1.2 Reach a rock outcropping to the left (north) that provides a nice view of the Sandia Mountains to the north.

1.8 The trail begins to descend after a steady climb.

2.2 Come to an intersection with the Otero Canyon Trail. Turn around and return via the same trail.

4.4 Arrive back at the trailhead parking area.

RIDE INFORMATION

Local Attractions/Events

The Museum of Archaeology & Material Culture, 22 Calvary Rd., Cedar Crest; (505) 281-2005; www.turquoisetrail.org/stops/detail/the-museum-of-archaeology-material-culture

Tinkertown Museum, 121 Sandia Crest Rd., Sandia Park; (505) 281-5233; http://tinkertown.com

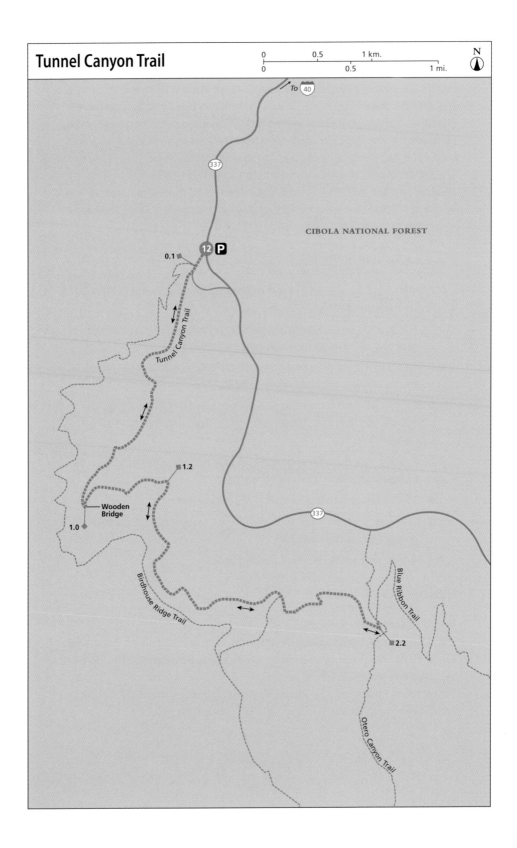

Local Bike Shops

The Bike Coop, 120 Yale Blvd. SE, Albuquerque; (505) 265-5170; www.bike coop.com

The Bike Smith, 901 Rio Grande Blvd. NW, Albuquerque; (505) 242-9253; www.thebikesmith.com

Routes, Rentals, and Tours, 404 San Filipe St. NW, Albuquerque; (505) 933-5667; http://routesrentals.com

Trek Bicycle Superstore, 5000 Menaul Blvd. NE, Albuquerque; (505) 312-7243; www.trekbicyclesuperstore.com

Two Wheel Drive, 1706 Central Ave. SE, Albuquerque; (505) 243-8443; www .twowheeldrive.com

Restaurants

El Pinto Restaurant and Cantina, 10500 4th St. NW, Albuquerque; (505) 898-1771; www.elpinto.com

Frontier Restaurant, 2400 Central Ave. SE, Albuquerque; (505) 266-0550; www.frontierrestaurant.com

Taj Mahal, 1430 Carlisle Blvd. NE, Albuquerque; (505) 255-1994; www.taj mahalcuisineofindia.com

13

Coyote and Chamisoso Trails Loop

Stretching for almost 11 miles, the Coyote and Chamisoso Trails are part of the Manzanita Mountains Trail System, nestled within the boundaries of the Cibola National Forest. The Coyote and Chamisoso Trails are technical and full of curvy, tight singletrack turns throughout. Located just minutes east of Albuquerque, these super fun trails are a great place to get your biking fix after work or on your weekend outing.

Start: Coyote Trailhead and Picnic Area

Length: 10.9-mile loop

Riding time: 2 to 2.5 hours

Best bike: Mountain bike

Terrain and trail surface: Mostly smooth; some very rocky uphill singletrack sections

Traffic and hazards: Motorcycles are allowed on the Manzanita Mountains Trail System, including the Chamisoso and Coyote Trails.

Maps: USDA Cibola National Forest—Sandia Ranger District, 2006; free Manzanita Mountain Trail System maps available at the Sandia Ranger Station in Tijeras

Trail contacts: Cibola National Forest—Sandia Ranger District, 11776 Hwy. 337, Tijeras 87059; (505) 281-3304; www.fs.usda.gov/detail/cibola/home

Special considerations: The trails may be accessed sunrise to sunset. Restrooms and a picnic area are located at the trailhead. Motorcycles use the area, but riders are very considerate to cyclists.

Getting there: Traveling I-40 East from Albuquerque, take exit 175 to Tijeras; veer right and continue straight at the four-way intersection to NM 337. Pass the Sandia Ranger Station on the left and continue 0.8

mile to FR 462. Turn left onto FR 462 and continue up the gravel road for 0.6 mile to the Coyote Trailhead and Picnic Area, on the left. **GPS:** N35 03.846' / W106 22.286'

THE RIDE

The Coyote and Chamisoso Trails are a great example of just how diverse mountain biking is in Albuquerque. These trails offer soaring views of the Sandia District. as well as wind through arroyos and glide through sweeping canyons that offer piñon-covered shade. Everything from technical and rocky uphill sections to super fun downhill sections will keep you on your toes while you ride. Coyote and Chamisoso are also great trails to escape to when temperatures begin to soar in Albuquerque during the dry summer months. Remember to bring extra water when on these trails, and practice caution while riding—these trails can be heavily used by motorbikes.

Leave the parking area and locate the trailhead for Coyote-Chamisoso Link (#05620). The link is located to the right of the locked gate that prevents unpermitted vehicles from continuing on FR 462. This gate remains locked at all times and is only accessible by trucks or cars if you have a permit. Bikes and motorcycles are allowed on FR 462.

Once you are at the Coyote-Chamisoso Trailhead, go through the gate and continue straight until the trail splits at 0.3 mile. Stay left at the split; the unmarked trail on the right is an unofficial shortcut that has been cut through the vegetation by other users. Please stay on marked trails. Although the left at the split is longer, it offers some great views. At 0.5 arrive in an open and grassy meadow that offers views of the Sandias. As you continue on the link from the meadow, the trail begins to climb gradually. At 0.8 mile the trail takes a slight dip until you arrive at a four-way intersection at 0.9 mile. The unmarked trail on right is the shortcut trail that you passed at mile 0.3. The trail in front of you is the returning loop at the end of the ride. Turn left at this point onto the Coyote Trail #05619.

The Coyote Trail descends for a while, and you cross a small singletrack bridge over an arroyo at 1.2 miles. The descent is a fun roller coaster of a ride over loose rock. It is not until mile 1.5 that you begin to climb; then, at 1.7 miles, the climb gets even bigger on this rocky and rutted-out portion along the trail. Finally, at 2.0 miles, you round a corner and the trail opens to another sprawling meadow filled with cacti and some beautiful yellow flowers, depending on the season. This is also where the trail meets up with the Coyote Split Trail #05851 on the right, but continue straight. After the

The trail gently descends into the canyon.

meadow, at 2.1 miles the trail descends into the canyon. This section of down-hill is a very fun singletrack, full of twists and turns. It also lasts for about 0.5 mile. At 2.6 miles the trail begins a series of steep technical climbs. Many obstacles line the trail. If you are unsure of any of the obstacles, feel free to walk portions of this section. It isn't until 3.7 miles that the trail encounters another downhill section.

Benefits of Fires

Seeing public lands scarred by fires is a bummer, but it's not all bad news! Fire removes low-growing underbrush, cleans the forest floor of debris, opens it up to sunlight, and nourishes the soil. The reduced competition for nutrients allows established trees to grow stronger and healthier.

From mile 5.3 the trail descends until you reach a gate at FR 462. Continue straight across FR 462 and enter FR 13. Once on FR 13, stay right as you begin a gradual climb. At 5.9 miles be on the lookout for a gate to Delbert's Trail (#05622), on the right. Turn right onto Delbert's Trail. The trail descends and offers beautiful open views through the piñon trees. Be careful—the trail hugs the side of the mountain as it descends. The trail reaches the Chamisoso Trail, on the right, at 7.2 miles. Turn right onto Chamisoso and begin to descend into the beautiful forested canyon. The trail becomes flat and flows through the canyon.

At 9.5 miles turn right onto the Coyote-Chamisoso Link (#05620), and then cross FR 462 once more at 9.7 miles. At this point the trail continues straight across FR 462. Begin a very gradual uphill until the trail comes to a four-way intersection. You have arrived back to where the trail first met up with the Coyote Trail. The Coyote Trail is now on the right. Continue straight and retrace your route to the Coyote-Chamisoso Trailhead parking area.

MILES AND DIRECTIONS

0.0 Start from the parking area and locate the Coyote-Chamisoso Link (#05620), to the right of the locked gate. Go straight through the gate. Go straight on the Coyote-Chamisoso Link.

0.3 Stay left at the split where an unmarked trail veers to the right.

0.9 Turn left onto the Coyote Trail (#05619).

1.2 Cross a singletrack bridge over an arroyo.

2.0 Arrive at the Coyote Split (#05851), on the right; continue straight.

5.7 Cross a gate to FR 462 and continue straight across FR 462 onto FR 13. Keep right as you climb; look for a gate to Delbert's Trail (#05622), on the right.

5.9 Turn right at the gate to Delbert's Trail (#05622).

7.2 Take the Chamisoso Trail (#05184), on the right.

Coyote and Chamisoso Trails Loop

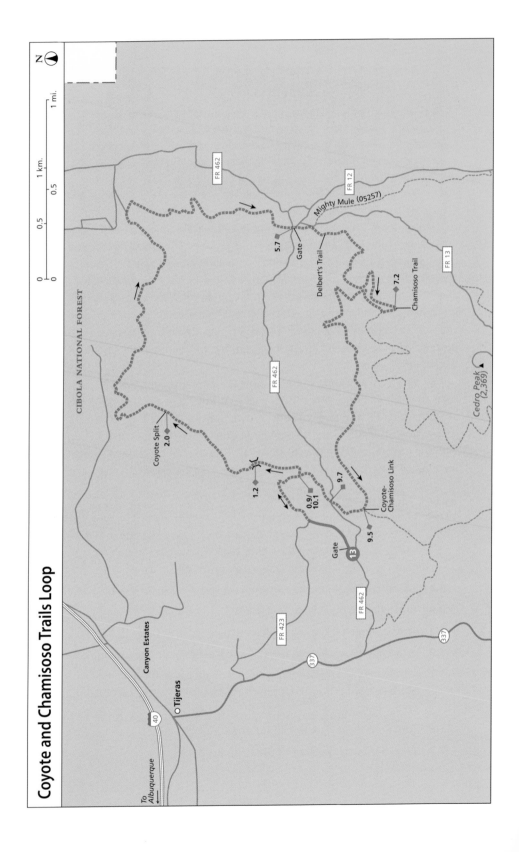

9.5 Turn right onto the Coyote-Chamisoso Link (#05620).

9.7 Cross FR 462 and continue straight on the Coyote-Chamisoso Link.

10.1 Continue straight as you pass the Coyote Trail (#05619), on the right.

10.9 Arrive back at the Coyote-Chamisoso Link Trailhead.

RIDE INFORMATION

Local Attractions/Events

The Museum of Archaeology & Material Culture, 22 Calvary Rd., Cedar Crest; (505) 281-2005; www.turquoisetrail.org/stops/detail/the-museum-of-archaeology-material-culture

Tinkertown Museum, 121 Sandia Crest Rd., Sandia Park; (505) 281-5233; http://tinkertown.com

Local Bike Shops

Bikeworks Albuquerque, 2839 Carlisle Blvd. NE, Albuquerque; (505) 884-0341; www.bikeworksabq.com

Cycle Cave, Inc., 5716 Menaul Blvd. NE, Albuquerque; (505) 884-6607

Fat Tire Cycles, 421 Montaño Rd. NE, Albuquerque; (505) 345-9005; www.fattirecycles.com

Performance Bicycle Shop, 1431 Mercantile Ave. NE, Albuquerque; (505) 765-2471; www.performancebike.com

REI, 1550 Mercantile Ave., Albuquerque; (505) 247-1191; www.REI.com

Sport Systems, 6915 Montgomery Blvd. NE, Albuquerque; (505) 837-9400; www.nmsportsystems.com

Restaurants

El Patio De Albuquerque, 142 Harvard Dr. SE, Albuquerque; (505) 268-4245; www.elpatiodealbuquerque.com

Monroe's, 6051 Osuna Rd. NE, Albuquerque; (505) 881-4224; www.monroeschile.com

Range Café, 4401 Wyoming Blvd. NE, Albuquerque; (505) 293-2633; www.rangecafe.com

Sandia Crest Road

The Sandia Crest Road is a scenic and challenging ride on the east side of the Sandia Mountains. The ride takes bikers to the highest point of the Sandia Mountains, meaning there is a significant amount of elevation gain on the ride up followed by a fast and fun descent.

Start: Sulphur Canyon Picnic Ground entrance and parking area

Length: 23.6 miles out and back

Riding time: 4 to 6 hours

Best bike: Road bike

Terrain and trail surface: Paved road; mostly uphill on the out portion and mostly downhill on the return; some sharp curves

Traffic and hazards: Motorized vehicles are permitted on the Sandia Crest Road, and the road can be busy during nice weather.

Maps: USGS Sandia Crest; road map available at the Sandia Ranger District visitor center

Trail contacts: Cibola National Forest—Sandia Ranger District, 11776 Hwy. 337, Tijeras 87059; (505) 281-3304; www.fs.usda.gov/main/cibola/home

Special considerations: Road may be snowy and icy during winter months.

Getting there: From Albuquerque take I-40 East to exit 175 toward NM 14/Cedar Crest. Stay left on NM 14 and continue north 6 miles to NM-536. Turn left (west) onto NM 536/Sandia Crest Road and continue 1.7 miles to the Sulphur Canyon Picnic Ground entrance. Turn left (west) into the picnic area and then make an immediate right (north) into the parking area. **GPS:** N35 10.178' / W106 23.027'

THE RIDE

The Sandia Crest Road bike ride tops out at 10,640 feet. This challenging but scenic climb to the highest point of the Sandia Mountains. The starting point for this ride offers riders over 4,000 feet of elevation gain, so get ready to work those thighs out. The descent is the highlight of the ride, and the scenery on the way down is not to be missed. Once on Sandia Crest Road you will be climbing mostly through a heavily forested area that sees mostly low but occasional heavy traffic. This is a great ride to enjoy in the early mornings and late afternoons of the summer months. There are several places to pull off along the ride and rest and/or picnic to make your ride enjoyable.

From the Sulphur Canyon Picnic Ground and parking area, turn left (north) and begin riding north on the Sandia Crest Road. The road surface on Sandia Crest is in good shape, but the shoulder area is pretty narrow. Traffic tends to be light on this road, but be careful. You will quickly pass the Doc Long Picnic Ground on the left (west) at 0.3 mile. This picnic area, like most

View of Sangre de Cristo Mountains from Sandia Crest Road

along the road, offers generous parking, restrooms, and great views. Continue riding as the road keeps climbing up the east side of the Sandia Mountains and pass the Tree Spring Trailhead parking area at 3.8 miles.

After a short winding stretch of road, you come to a nice downhill break. Relax and cruise on down as the road passes the Sandia Peak ski area on the left (west) at 5.2 miles. After the ski area, the road begins to climb again. During this climb you'll pass the Balsam Glade Picnic Area on your right (east) at 5.7 miles. NM 165 can also be accessed from this point. NM 165 is a dirt and rock road that circles around to the north end of the Sandias and goes to the small artist town of Placitas.

Continue riding as the road begins heading west and becomes steeper. Pass the Capulin Picnic Area and winter fun park on your right (north) at 6.3 miles and then ride through a series of switchbacks. Watch for dirt and loose gravel on the turns here, especially on your descent. At 9.6 miles you pass the 10K Trail south trailhead on your left (south) and the 10K Trail north trailhead on your right (north). There is a restroom at the 10K Trail north trailhead parking area. Just up the road you pass the Ellis Trailhead parking area on your left (south) at 10.5 miles. There's just one switchback left as you continue the ascent and arrive at the Sandia Peak summit at 11.8 miles. At the summit are great views and a visitor center. After enjoying your success and the rewards, return to the Sulphur Canyon Picnic Ground and parking area via the same route for a round-trip of 23.6 miles.

MILES AND DIRECTIONS

0.0 Start from the Sulphur Canyon Picnic Ground and parking area and begin riding north on the Sandia Crest Road.

0.3 Pass the Doc Long Picnic Ground on the left (west).

3.8 Ride past the Tree Spring Trailhead parking area on the left (west).

5.2 After a short downhill, pass the Sandia Peak ski area on the left (west).

5.7 Pass the Balsam Glade Picnic Area on the right (east).

6.3 Pass the Capulin Picnic Area on the right (east).

7.2 The road continues to climb, and switchbacks begin as you pass the 9 Mile Picnic Area on the left (south).

9.6 Ride past the 10K Trail south parking area (left) and north parking area (right).

10.5 Pass the Ellis Trailhead parking area (left).

Sandia Crest Road

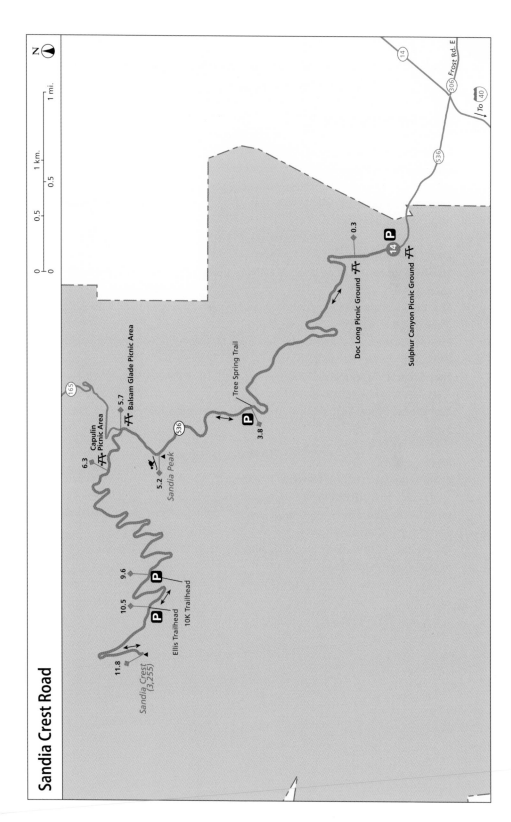

11.8 Reach the Sandia Peak summit. Return the way you came.

23.6 Arrive back at the Sulphur Canyon Picnic Ground and parking area.

RIDE INFORMATION

Local Attractions/Events
Elena Gallegos Picnic Area, 7100 Tramway Blvd. NE, Albuquerque; (505) 857-8334; www.cabq.gov/openspace/elenagallegos.html
Sandia Peak ski area, Mile Marker 6, Hwy. 536, Sandia Park; (505) 242-9052; http://sandiapeak.com

Local Bike Shops
The Bike Coop, 120 Yale Blvd. SE, Albuquerque; (505) 265-5170; www.bikecoop.com
The Bike Smith, 901 Rio Grande Blvd. NW, Albuquerque; (505) 242-9253; www.thebikesmith.com
Routes, Rentals, and Tours, 404 San Filipe St. NW, Albuquerque; (505) 933-5667; http://routesrentals.com
Trek Bicycle Superstore, 5000 Menaul Blvd. NE, Albuquerque; (505) 312-7243; www.trekbicyclesuperstore.com
Two Wheel Drive, 1706 Central Ave. SE, Albuquerque; (505) 243-8443; www.twowheeldrive.com

Restaurants
El Pinto Restaurant and Cantina, 10500 4th St. NW, Albuquerque; (505) 898-1771; www.elpinto.com
Frontier Restaurant, 2400 Central Ave. SE, Albuquerque; (505) 266-0550; www.frontierrestaurant.com
Taj Mahal, 1430 Carlisle Blvd. NE, Albuquerque; (505) 255-1994; www.tajmahalcuisineofindia.com

Tree Spring Trail

The Tree Spring Trail is a popular trail in the Sandia Mountains. Riders can reach the 10K Trail via the Tree Spring Trail without having to drive farther up the Sandia Crest Road to the 10K parking area. This 3.6-mile out-and-back ride will take you up the gradual ascent to the 10K Trail, where you can return via the same route or explore the 10K Trail.

Start: Tree Spring Trailhead parking area, on the west side of Sandia Crest Road

Length: 3.6 miles out and back

Riding time: 1 to 2 hours

Best bike: Mountain bike

Terrain and trail surface: Dirt packed singletrack the entire route. The trail ascends steadily and then is all downhill on the return.

Traffic and hazards: No motorized vehicles are permitted on the trail. Riders may encounter hikers and trail runners.

Maps: USGS Sandia Crest; trail map available at the Sandia Ranger District visitor center

Trail contacts: Cibola National Forest—Sandia Ranger District, 11776 Hwy. 337, Tijeras 87059; (505) 281-3304; www.fs.usda.gov/main/cibola/home

Special considerations: Trail may be snowy and icy in the winter. Parking area may be closed after heavy snow.

Getting there: From Albuquerque, take I-40 East to exit 175 toward NM 14/Cedar Crest. Stay left on NM 14 and continue north 6 miles to NM 536. Turn left (west) onto NM 536/Sandia Crest Road and continue 6.3 miles to the Tree Spring Trailhead parking area, on the left (west). **GPS:** N35 11.620' / W106 24.285'

THE RIDE

The Tree Spring Trail, on the east side of the Sandia Mountains, sees heavy use throughout spring, summer, and fall. The trail also sees a good bit of use by snowshoers during the winter months. As far as rides up the Sandia Mountains go, the Tree Spring Trail offers one of the easier climbs; it gains only about 880 vertical feet, with only a few short steep ascents.

The Tree Spring Trail got its name from a spring that flows from under a tree stump about 0.5 mile down the road before you reach the Tree Spring Trailhead parking area. The parking area here can be busy in the warmer months, especially summer. Parking isn't usually an issue in winter unless heavy snows cause snowplows to move snow into the parking area.

From the Tree Spring Trail parking area, locate the trailhead sign near the southwest end of the parking lot. Pit toilets are available if nature should call before you begin your ride. Begin riding on the packed dirt trail as it starts a steady ascent up the east side of the Sandia Mountains. After 0.3 mile you

Tree Spring Trailhead

reach a junction with the Oso Corredor Trail. Stay right (southwest) on the Tree Spring Trail.

Continue the slow and steady climb up the Tree Spring Trail and come to a nice rest area at 0.5 mile on the right (north). The spot is clear of vegetation and has a few big boulders to sit on; a view of the Sandias makes the spot quite nice for a quick break. The trail continues its climb for the next 0.5 mile through the ponderosa pine and spruce forest. At 1.0 mile the trail makes a sharp right (northwest) turn and begins a slightly steeper ascent for a short a distance before reaching another ideal resting place on the right (east) at 1.2 miles.

After a short break, begin riding north and then west again as the trail continues to climb. At 1.8 miles the Tree Spring Trail intersects the 10K Trail. Some riders may wish to turn left (west) onto the 10K Trail and ride a short distance to the South Crest Trail for a few views west of the Sandias. For this ride description, turn around at the Tree Spring and 10K Trail junction to return to the trailhead via the same route you just ascended for a round-trip of 3.6 miles.

MILES AND DIRECTIONS

0.0 Start from the Tree Spring Trailhead and begin riding west.

0.3 Reach an intersection with the Oso Corredor Trail. Stay right (southwest) on the Tree Spring Trail.

0.5 Come to an area that offers a nice resting place and view of the Sandias on the right (north).

1.0 The trail makes a sharp right (northwest) turn. Continue on a fairly steep ascent here.

1.2 Reach another opening that offers a nice view of the eastern side of the Sandias.

1.8 The Tree Spring Trail meets the 10K Trail. Turn around and return to the trailhead via the same route.

3.6 Arrive back at the trailhead.

RIDE INFORMATION

Local Attractions/Events
Gutierrez Canyon Open Space, Cedar Crest (call Open Space Division for directions); (505) 452-5200; www.cabq.gov/parksandrecreation/open-space/lands/east-mountain-open-space

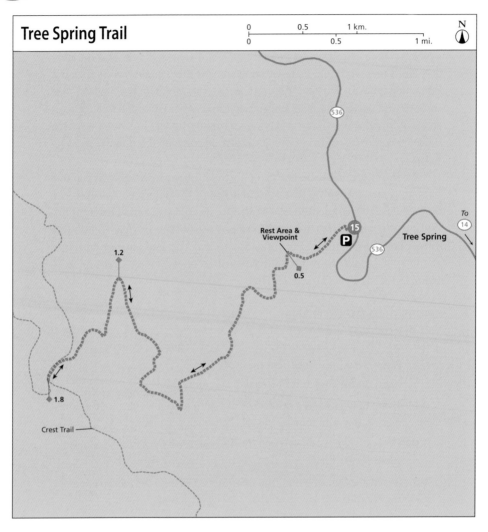

Tree Spring Trail

0   0.5   1 km.
0   0.5   1 mi.

N

536

Rest Area &
Viewpoint

15

P

536

Tree Spring

To **14**

1.2

0.5

1.8

Crest Trail

Sandia Peak ski area, Mile Marker 6, Hwy. 536, Sandia Park; (505) 242-9052; http://sandiapeak.com

Local Bike Shops

Bikeworks Albuquerque, 2839 Carlisle Blvd. NE, Albuquerque; (505) 884-0341; www.bikeworksabq.com

Cycle Cave, Inc., 5716 Menaul Blvd. NE, Albuquerque; (505) 884-6607

Fat Tire Cycles, 421 Montaño Rd. NE, Albuquerque; (505) 345-9005; www.fat tirecycles.com

Performance Bicycle Shop, 1431 Mercantile Ave. NE, Albuquerque; (505) 765-2471; www.performancebike.com

REI, 1550 Mercantile Ave., Albuquerque; (505) 247-1191; www.REI.com

Sport Systems, 6915 Montgomery Blvd. NE, Albuquerque; (505) 837-9400; www.nmsportsystems.com

Restaurants

El Patio De Albuquerque, 142 Harvard Dr. SE, Albuquerque; (505) 268-4245; www.elpatiodealbuquerque.com

Monroe's, 6051 Osuna Rd. NE, Albuquerque; (505) 881-4224; www.monroes chile.com

Range Café, 4401 Wyoming Blvd. NE, Albuquerque; (505) 293-2633; www .rangecafe.com

10K and Ellis Trails Loop

Many of the trails in the Sandia Mountains do not allow mountain biking because they are located in the wilderness area. The 10K and Ellis Trails Loop is one of the exceptions, as the trails run right along the wilderness border. Most other traffic on the trails is foot traffic, but mountain bikers do not want to miss out on this fun loop.

Start: Northwest corner of the 10K Trail north trailhead parking area

Length: 5.0-mile loop

Riding time: 1 to 2 hours

Best bike: Mountain bike

Terrain and trail surface: Packed dirt singletrack and short section on paved road; long downhill section followed by ups and downs and then downhill on the road

Traffic and hazards: Riders may encounter hikers and equestrians on the singletrack and motorized vehicles on the road.

Maps: USGS Sandia Crest; trail map available at the Sandia Ranger District visitor center

Trail contacts: USGS Sandia Crest; trail map available at the Sandia Ranger District visitor center

Trail contacts: Cibola National Forest—Sandia Ranger District, 11776 Hwy. 337, Tijeras 87059; (505) 281-3304; www.fs.usda.gov/main/cibola/home

Special considerations: Watch for motorized vehicles on the road section of this ride; the curves may cause impaired vision.

Getting there: From Albuquerque, take I-40 East to exit 175 toward NM 14/Cedar Crest. Stay left on NM 14 and continue north 6 miles to NM

536. Turn left (west) onto NM 536/Sandia Crest Road and continue 11.3 miles to the 10K Trail north trailhead parking area, on the right (north). **GPS:** N35 20.975' / W106 43.532'

THE RIDE

The rides in the Sandia Mountains are unique for first-time riders. Riders starting in Albuquerque can gain well over 5,000 feet of elevation in a relatively

Small footbridge near 10K Trailhead

short distance as they travel to the highest point of the Sandias, Sandia Peak. The 10K and Ellis Trail sections described here are at one of the higher elevations in the Sandias, where mountain biking is permitted on the trails. Located just a short distance from the summit of the mountain, the parking area here provides hikers and riders great access to the trail system.

Locate the trail at the northwest corner of the parking area and begin riding northwest on the north section of the 10K Trail. The trail here is packed dirt singletrack and has a lot of exposed roots. The trail quickly begins descending and you pass a great little area to pull over and take in views to the east at 0.5 mile. Continue riding north as the trail descends and hits a few steep descents as well as a few tight and technical areas. Encounter one short uphill around 0.9 mile and then reach a trail junction at 2.0 miles.

Turn left (northwest) to stay on the 10K Trail. Right (northeast) is the Osha Trail. After a short uphill you arrive at another trail junction at 2.2 miles. Turn left (south) here onto the Ellis Trail. Right (north) is also the Ellis Trail, which continues north; the 10K Trail continues straight (northwest). After turning left (south) onto the Ellis Trail, you ride through an open meadow as the trail eventually becomes a mix of rocky and packed-dirt surface. Continue on a series of ups and downs as the trail continues south. At 3.5 miles the single-track trail ends and joins a doubletrack trail. The trail gradually turns southeast and slowly climbs until you reach the Sandia Crest Road at 4.1 miles. Turn left (southeast) onto the Sandia Crest Road and ride down the road. Watch for loose dirt and gravel on the curves. At 5.0 miles return to the trailhead and parking area on the left (north).

MILES AND DIRECTIONS

0.0 Start at the northwest corner of the parking area and begin riding northwest on the 10K Trail.

0.5 Enjoy a nice view to the east.

2.0 Turn left (northwest) at the trail junction to stay on the 10K Trail. Right (northeast) is the Osha Trail.

2.2 Turn left (south) onto the Ellis Trail. Right (north) is also the Ellis Trail; the 10K Trail continues straight (northwest).

3.5 The singletrack ends; the trail continues on doubletrack.

4.1 Turn left (southeast) onto Sandia Crest Road.

5.0 Arrive back at the 10K Trail north trailhead parking area.

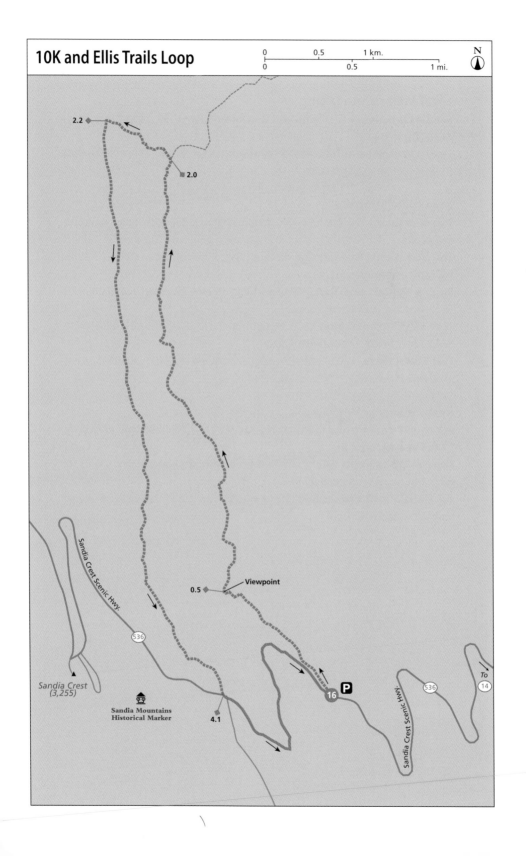

10K and Ellis Trails Loop

0   0.5   1 km.

0   0.5   1 mi.

N

2.2

2.0

Viewpoint

0.5

Sandia Crest Scenic Hwy.

536

Sandia Crest
(3,255)

Sandia Mountains
Historical Marker

4.1

16

P

Sandia Crest Scenic Hwy.

536

To

14

RIDE INFORMATION

Local Attractions/Events

Sandia Crest House Gift Shop and Restaurant, Hwy. 536, Sandia Park; (505) 243-0605

Sandia Peak Ski and Tramway, 30 Tramway Rd. NE, Albuquerque; (505) 856-7325; http://sandiapeak.com

Local Bike Shops

The Bike Coop, 120 Yale Blvd. SE, Albuquerque; (505) 265-5170; www.bikecoop.com

The Bike Smith, 901 Rio Grande Blvd. NW, Albuquerque; (505) 242-9253; www.thebikesmith.com

Routes, Rentals, and Tours, 404 San Filipe St. NW, Albuquerque; (505) 933-5667; http://routesrentals.com

Trek Bicycle Superstore, 5000 Menaul Blvd. NE, Albuquerque; (505) 312-7243; www.trekbicyclesuperstore.com

Two Wheel Drive, 1706 Central Ave. SE, Albuquerque; (505) 243-8443; www.twowheeldrive.com

Restaurants

El Pinto Restaurant and Cantina, 10500 4th St. NW, Albuquerque; (505) 898-1771; www.elpinto.com

Frontier Restaurant, 2400 Central Ave. SE, Albuquerque; (505) 266-0550; www.frontierrestaurant.com

Taj Mahal, 1430 Carlisle Blvd. NE, Albuquerque; (505) 255-1994; www.tajmahalcuisineofindia.com

North of Albuquerque

Jemez Dam Road (Ride 17)

The land north of Albuquerque offers cyclists a rugged yet enchanting network of trails. The ever-changing beauty of the landscape north of Albuquerque is the reason so many visitors flock to New Mexico. From the sparkling white gypsum trails found just outside San Ysidro to the many natural hot springs throughout the Jemez Mountains, the area's vast openness and unique landscapes offer visitors a tranquil and relaxed retreat from the daily hustle of the Metro Area.

Jemez Dam Road

The ride to Jemez Dam is an enjoyable cruise just north of Albuquerque that offers great views of the Sandia Mountains. Riders will arrive at an overlook of Jemez Canyon and the engineering wonder of the Jemez Canyon Dam. The area is rich with both modern-day and historical attractions.

Start: Santa Ana Star Casino parking area

Length: 12.4 miles out and back

Riding time: 2 to 3 hours

Best bike: Road bike

Terrain and trail surface: Paved road; mostly flat with one descent and climb in and out of a canyon

Traffic and hazards: Riders should expect to encounter motorized vehicles. Watch for cattleguard crossings.

Map: USGS Santa Ana Pueblo

Trail contacts: US Army Corps of Engineers, 82 Dam Crest Rd., Pena Blanca 87041; (505) 465-0307; www.spa.usace.army.mil/Missions/CivilWorks/Recreation/JemezCanyonDam.aspx

Special considerations: Day use is restricted to the immediate developed areas.

Getting there: From Albuquerque take I-25 North to exit 242 and turn left (west) onto US 550. Drive 2.1 miles and turn right (north) onto James Dam Road/Jemez Dam Road and into the Santa Ana Star Casino parking area. **GPS:** N35 33.417' / W106 56.606'

THE RIDE

The Jemez Canyon Dam is located in an ecological area known as plains-mesa sand scrub. The plants that grow in this area can survive in deep sands. Environmental conditions such as low precipitation and rocky, sandy, and gravelly soils are contributing factors to the formation of this type of vegetation community. This area also supports a diverse array of animal species. Townsend ground squirrel, dark kangaroo mouse, and sagebrush vole all call

Jemez Dam

this area home. Coyotes and foxes can also be seen here. Common reptile species include the leopard lizard, collared lizard, and western diamondback rattlesnake.

In addition to the unique vegetation and wildlife here, there are 103 archaeological sites on Pueblo of Santa Ana Reservation, including the historic Tamaya village. The village is listed on the State Register of Cultural Properties and on the National Register of Historic Places.

From the Santa Ana Casino parking area, begin riding north on James Dam Road/Jemez Dam Road and then turn right (north) onto Tamaya Boulevard at 0.3 mile. The road here is nice and wide, with ample shoulder space for riding. At 1.3 miles the shoulder space ends and the road becomes a tighter two-lane road, but with very little traffic. Cross through the Jemez Canyon Dam gate at 1.7 miles and continue riding north, with great views of the Sandia Mountains back to the southeast.

Cross cattleguards at 3.6 miles and at 4.2 miles, just before the road descends into Jemez Canyon. At 4.8 miles you reach the canyon floor and pass a couple of research stations before beginning your ascent back up and out of the canyon. The road curves east as you come out of the canyon and an Army Corps of Engineer sign sits on the right (north) side of the road at 5.8 miles. Not long after the sign, you arrive at the dam overlook and day-use area at 6.2 miles. Picnic tables, shelters, and restrooms are available here. Return to the parking area via the same route for a round-trip of 12.4 miles.

MILES AND DIRECTIONS

0.0 Start from the casino parking area and begin riding north on James Dam Road/Jemez Dam Road.

0.3 Turn right onto Tamaya Boulevard.

1.7 Arrive at the Jemez Dam Road gate.

3.6 Cross a cattleguard.

4.2 Cross a second cattleguard.

4.8 Reach the bottom of Jemez Canyon.

5.8 Pass the Jemez Dam Army Corps of Engineers sign.

6.2 Reach the Jemez Dam overlook and day use area. Return the way you came.

12.4 Arrive back at the casino parking area.

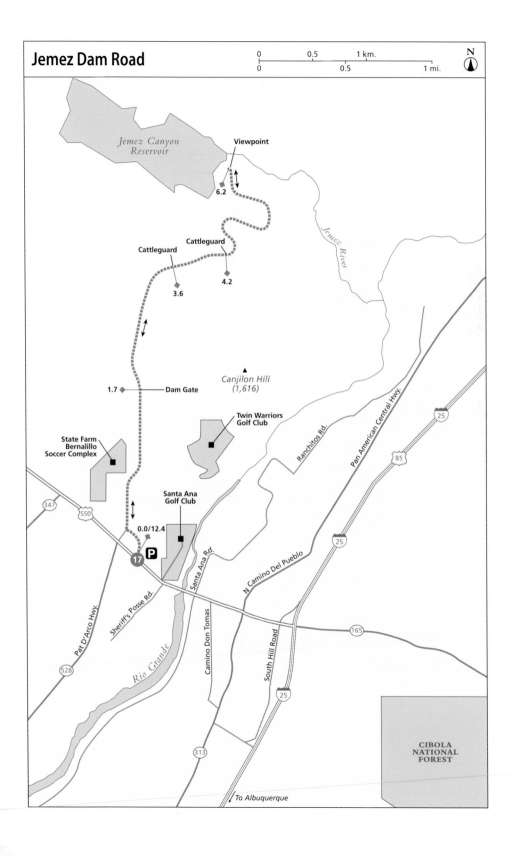

Jemez Dam Road

0   0.5   1 km.

0   0.5   1 mi.

N

Jemez Canyon
Reservoir

Viewpoint

6.2

Jemez River

Cattleguard

Cattleguard

3.6

4.2

Canjilon Hill
(1,616)

1.7   Dam Gate

Twin Warriors
Golf Club

State Farm
Bernalillo
Soccer Complex

Santa Ana
Golf Club

0.0/12.4

Ranchitos Rd.

Pan American Central Hwy.

25

85

25

17   P

Pat D'Arco Hwy.

Sheriff's Posse Rd.

Rio Grande

347

550

Santa Ana Rd.

Camino Don Tomas

N. Camino Del Pueblo

South Hill Road

25

165

25

528

313

CIBOLA
NATIONAL
FOREST

To Albuquerque

RIDE INFORMATION

Local Attractions/Events

Bandelier National Monument, 15 Entrance Rd., Los Alamos; (505) 672-3861; www.nps.gov/band/index.htm

Tetilla Lake Recreation Area, 82 Dam Crest Rd., Pena Blanca; (505) 465-0307; www.reserveamerica.com/campgroundDetails.do?subTabIndex=0&&contractCode=nrso&parkCode=tpea

Local Bike Shops

The Broken Spoke, 1426 Cerrillos Rd., Santa Fe; (505) 992-3102; http://broken spokesantafe.com

New Mexico Bike and Sport, 524 W Cordova Rd., Santa Fe; (505) 820-0809; http://nmbikensport.com

Rob and Charlie's, 1632 St. Michaels Dr., Santa Fe; (505) 471-9119; www.robandcharlies.com

Restaurants

Cafe Pasqual's, 121 Don Gaspar Ave., Santa Fe; (505) 983-9340; www.pasquals.com

The Cowgirl, 319 S Guadalupe St., Santa Fe; (505) 982-2465; www.cowgirl santafe.com

La Casa Sena La Cantina, 125 E Palace Ave., Santa Fe; (505) 988-9232; www.lacasasena.com

White Ridge Bike Trails Loop

The White Ridge Bike Trails, formerly known as the White Mesa Trails, are a hidden geologist's, paleontologist's, and mountain biker's dream. Located just a short drive north of Albuquerque and just minutes outside San Ysidro, the White Ridge area is known for its unique white gypsum trails, hence the name White Ridge. Everything from fossils to petrified trees and exposed ridgelines can be found in the White Ridge Trails area.

Start: White Ridge Bike Trails parking area

Length: 7.5-mile loop

Riding time: 2 hours

Best bike: Mountain bike

Terrain and trail surface: Moderate with smooth gypsum singletrack; some hike-a-bike rocky areas

Traffic and hazards: Expect technical downhills and exposed ridges in the first 2 miles. Hikers and other cyclists use the trail; equestrians are allowed only on junctions #24 and #6.

Maps: USGS White Ridge; detailed trail map and brochure available at the trailhead and on the website

Trail contacts: Bureau of Land Management, Rio Puerco Field Office, 435 Montaño Rd. NE, Albuquerque 77107; (505) 761-8700; www.blm.gov/nm/st/en/prog/recreation/rio_puerco/white_mesa_bike_trails.html

Special considerations: Bring extra water. There are no water sources available on the trails, and summer temperatures can get extreme.

Getting there: From Albuquerque, take I-25 North to exit 242 for Bernalillo. Turn left and drive north on US 550 for about 20 miles and then turn left onto Cabezon Rd (CR 906). Immediately veer left at the split in the road, keeping straight onto Cabezon Road the entire way. Drive 4.4 miles to the White Ridge Bike Trails parking area, on the right. **GPS:** N35 40.113' / W106 50.485'

THE RIDE

The White Ridge Bike Trails area winds through Pueblo of Zia, State of New Mexico, and Bureau of Land Management (BLM) land. It was with the cooperation of multiple land agencies that the White Ridge Trails area was developed especially for mountain biking use. With that said, many colleges and universities also travel here to study the history of the land. As remote as the White Ridge area is, trails can be busy around trail junction (TJ) #21. The rest of the area sees less use.

From the White Ridge Trails parking area, which offers shaded picnic tables, locate the trailhead in the back corner of the lot, next to the information board. As you begin biking up this small canyon, stay left in 200 feet as you arrive at junction 1.

After this first junction, the trail continues to curve to the left as you make your initial climb and pass TJ #2. There will be a heavily used singletrack at 0.2 mile on the left of the trail between TJs #2 and #3. Stay straight and bear left around a small gypsum wall until you reach junction 3.

When you arrive at TJ #3 at the 0.3-mile mark, you will notice the Tierra Amarilla anticline in front of you. The anticline, also known as the Dragon's Back, is a very fun and technical bike trail. Turn right at TJ #3 and note the large gypsum summit in the near distance; this summit is where you will find TJ #21. Keep right as you climb away from the edges of the Dragon's Back. Dozens of trails have been cut through this area, and a bit of route finding may be required on this section of the trail.

Once you have arrived at TJ #21 at 0.7 mile, there is a great viewpoint on top of the gypsum knob directly in front of you. At this point the trail meanders slightly to the left of the gypsum knob until you reach TJ #22 at the 0.8-mile mark. This is also the beginning of the Center Spine. Go straight at this point, being cautious as you ride along the ridge of the spine. There are many loose rocks and not a lot of room for error.

As you travel down the spine, you will bike into a small sandy pit at 1.0 mile; go straight out of the sandy pit and keep right. At 1.1 miles there is a very steep 10-foot drop. It would be wise to hike your bike down this pathway. There are many rocks alongside the trail that will help you keep your footing as you hike your bike down this steep drop. When you near the end of the Center Spine at 1.3 miles, the trail becomes a smooth singletrack and there is an abrupt technical downhill. The trail splits as you descend this downhill; keep right. Once the trail has left the Center Spine, you bike into an open grassy plateau before beginning a moderate climb.

At 1.9 miles stop for a moment. The trail passes a picturesque mineral-water spring—not something you would expect to see in the middle of this desolate area. Water freely flows from this small blue hole in the ground, and minerals deposit a multitude of colors outlining the ground's surface. Arrive at TJ #12 at 2.3 miles; continue straight at this point and then bear left. Keep an eye out for TJ #11 on the left—it may sneak up on you during the descent. At TJ #11 you ascend a small hill. Once at the top of this ascent, at 2.6 miles, look to your right; the trail traverses directly over a gypsum dome until you reach TJ #10.

At 2.7 miles reach TJ #10 and continue straight up a singletrack on a small hill. On this section you pass a large sinkhole on your right. The sinkhole is a

A beautiful sunset view from the White Ridge Trails

remnant of an old mineral spring. Sometimes after a heavy rain, the sinkhole may fill with water, but it is usually dried up. As you continue on the trail, at 3.2 miles you start to descend. The trail may be washed out at this point and covered with white gypsum deposits. To stay on the trail, descend and bear left. Once you have located the trail at the bottom of the descent, keep left.

Once you have passed TJ #9 at 3.4 miles, keep left in 100 feet and start an ascent on the doubletrack. This will take you back to TJ #10. When you reach TJ #10, at 4.2 miles, continue straight up the doubletrack until you arrive at junction 11. As you pass TJ #11 on your right, continue straight on the doubletrack. The doubletrack becomes level for easy biking as you reach TJ #12. At 4.5 miles pass TJ #12 on your right and continue left on the road. At 4.8 miles pass TJ #13 on the right; continue straight and take the next road on right, which is unmarked.

At 5.1 miles there is a fun and easy ride on the right called Final Frontier. Gliding through this section, you arrive at TJ #16 at 5.5 miles. Turn right at TJ #16 and bike out to an exposed viewpoint. This gives you an opportunity to see the trail you've ridden from a different perspective, and the trail is quite exhilarating. Once you have reached the viewpoint at 5.6 miles, turn around and backtrack to TJ #16. Turn right at the junction.

Reach TJ #17 at mile 6.5; keep right. As you round a bend at 6.6 miles, you pass TJ #18 on your left. Keep straight on the trail and ascend until you reach TJ #19 on your right. Proceed straight at this point until you reach the bottom of the gypsum knob, where you will find TJ #21 on your left. This is where you first began the loop. Retrace your original path as you descend back to the parking lot at 7.5 miles.

MILES AND DIRECTIONS

0.0 Start from the parking area at the main trailhead sign and veer left in about 200 feet at TJ #1.

0.2 Keep straight at TJ #2 till you arrive at TJ #3.

0.3 Arrive at TJ #3; turn right.

0.7 Reach TJ #21; go straight for 100 feet till you arrive at the bottom of the gypsum hill in front of you. Turn left and follow the hill down to the right to TJ #22.

0.8 Arrive onto the Center Spine, TJ #22 go straight.

1.1 There is a 10-foot drop at this section. It's time to hike-a-bike.

1.3 Come to a very steep singletrack; stay right at the split.

2.3 At TJ #12 go straight and stay left.

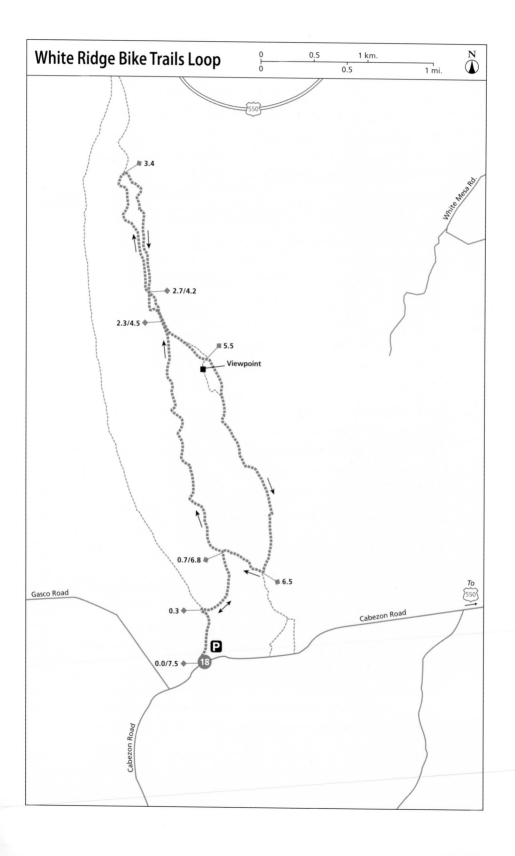

White Ridge Bike Trails Loop

0   0.5   1 km.

0   0.5   1 mi.

N

550

White Mesa Rd.

3.4

2.7/4.2

2.3/4.5

5.5

Viewpoint

0.7/6.8

6.5

Gasco Road

0.3

To 550

Cabezon Road

P

18

0.0/7.5

Cabezon Road

2.5 TJ #11is a sharp turn to the left. Keep an eye out for this one.

2.6 Turn right and ride straight over this gypsum dome.

2.7 Reach TJ #10 and go straight to a singletrack located on the hill.

3.1 Arrive at an opening and stay left to follow the trail.

3.2 The trail may be washed out at this point. Keep descending and locate the trail on the left.

3.4 Arrive at TJ #9. Go straight and keep left in 100 feet.

4.2 Arrive back at TJ #10 and keep straight on the road.

4.3 Pass TJ #11 on the right.

4.5 Arrive at TJ #12. Keep left on the road.

4.8 Pass TJ #13. Keep straight and then take the next road on the right.

5.1 Take the trail on right titled Final Frontier.

5.5 At TJ #16 turn right to the viewpoint.

5.6 Arrive at the viewpoint. Turn around and backtrack to TJ #16.

5.8 Arrive back at TJ #16; turn right.

6.5 Keep right at TJ # 17 onto singletrack.

6.6 Pass TJ #18; keep straight.

6.7 Pass TJ #19; keep straight.

6.8 Turn left onto TJ #21 and retrace your path to the trailhead.

7.5 Arrive back at the White Ridge Bike Trails parking area.

RIDE INFORMATION

Local Attractions/Events
Bandelier National Monument, 15 Entrance Rd., Los Alamos; (505) 672-3861; www.nps.gov/band/index.htm
Cochiti Lake Recreation Area, 82 Dam Crest Rd., Pena Blanca; (505) 465-0307; www.recreation.gov/recAreaDetails.do?contractCode=NRSO&recAreaI d=485&agencyCode=130

Local Bike Shops
Bikeworks Albuquerque, 2839 Carlisle Blvd. NE, Albuquerque; (505) 884-0341; www.bikeworksabq.com
Cycle Cave, Inc., 5716 Menaul Blvd. NE, Albuquerque; (505) 884-6607
Fat Tire Cycles, 421 Montaño Rd. NE, Albuquerque; (505) 345-9005; www.fat tirecycles.com

Performance Bicycle Shop, 1431 Mercantile Ave. NE, Albuquerque; (505) 765-2471; www.performancebike.com

REI, 1550 Mercantile Ave., Albuquerque; (505) 247-1191; www.REI.com

Sport Systems, 6915 Montgomery Blvd. NE, Albuquerque; (505) 837-9400; www.nmsportsystems.com

Restaurants

El Patio De Albuquerque, 142 Harvard Dr. SE, Albuquerque; (505) 268-4245; www.elpatiodealbuquerque.com

Monroe's, 6051 Osuna Rd. NE, Albuquerque; (505) 881-4224; www.monroes chile.com

Range Café, 4401 Wyoming Blvd. NE, Albuquerque; (505) 293-2633; www .rangecafe.com

San Ysidro Trials Area Trail

The San Ysidro Trials Area Trail offers a beautiful ride to cyclists for most of the year. The only time riders cannot enjoy the area is the five or six times a year the New Mexico Trials Association (NMTA) holds motorbiking events on the trails. This 5.1-mile lollipop ride will take you on what appears to be a flat desert ride. The narrow canyons that can be explored at about 2 miles are the highlight of this ride.

Start: Trials Area parking lot on the north side of US 550

Length: 5.1-mile lollipop

Riding time: 2 hours

Best bike: Mountain bike

Terrain and trail surface: Dirt road; Dirt, sand, and rock singletrack

Traffic and hazards: No motorized vehicles are permitted on the trail except when the trail is closed to mountain bikers. Riders may encounter hikers and equestrians.

Map: USGS San Ysidro

Trail contacts: Bureau of Land Management, Rio Puerco Field Office, 435 Montaño Rd. NE, Albuquerque 87107; (505) 761-8700; www.blm .gov/nm/st/en/prog/recreation/rio_puerco/san_ysidro_trials_area.html

Special considerations: The area may be closed to riders during motorcycle trial periods. Check www.nmtrials.org for a list of events.

Getting there: From Albuquerque, take I-25 North to exit 242 toward US 550/Bernalillo. Turn left (west) onto US 550 and continue 25 miles to just past the weigh station on the northwest side of the town of San Ysidro. Turn right (north) into the signed San Ysidro Trials Area parking lot, just past the weigh station. **GPS:** N35 33.257' / W106 48.392'

THE RIDE

The San Ysidro Trails Area Trail offers a unique opportunity to ride a lollipop trail at the base of the southern start of the Rocky Mountains. The Nacimiento Mountains here and the Sangre de Cristos over near Santa Fe both get credit for being the southern tip of the Rocky Mountains, which run as far north as Alaska. In addition to getting credit for being the southern tip of the Rockies, the area also forms the southeast edge of the Colorado Plateau.

Slot Canyon

Slickrock along the San Ysidro Trials Area Trail

The Trials Area hosts about five dirt bike races each year. Don't be put off by the sound of this. Other than those five or so trials, motorized vehicles are not allowed in the area. For the most part you won't be able to tell that dirt bikes race through the area on the same trail you are about to ride. Mountain bikers tend to be drawn to the area because many hikers don't want to walk the 1.2 miles just to reach the main Trials Area parking.

From the roadside Trials Area parking lot, begin riding north on the dirt/sand road that leaves from the northwest corner of the parking area. Follow the road as it climbs a little and turns slightly northwest. Pass a fence at 0.5 mile with a sign on it that reads "San Ysidro Trials Area." Continue riding northwest and then north to the main Trials Area parking lot. In the middle of the dirt parking area is an information kiosk. The singletrack trail begins directly behind the kiosk (east). Cross a usually dry wash and begin riding northeast on the trail. This area can be a little confusing, as the sandy trail blends in with the rest of the landscape. If you keep heading in a northeast direction, you should be fine. At 1.6 miles you reach a fork in the trail. Stay left (northeast) at the fork and continue to make your way to the "Grand Canyon." Reach the canyon at 2.0 miles and turn right (south) to begin following the trail as it parallels the canyon. There are many spots along the trail where you can climb down into the slot canyon and explore. (**Note:** If you choose to climb down and explore the canyon, keep in mind that there are numerous water pools to cross.) Continue to follow the well-worn trail, marked with rock cairns along the canyon.

At 2.5 miles the canyon begins to open up and the trail drops down into the canyon for a short distance. The trail then makes a sharp right (southwest) out of the canyon at 2.6 miles and goes up and down several hills, crosses a wash at 3.1 miles, and crosses a few slickrock areas. At 3.9 miles the trail returns to the main Trials Area parking lot. Turn left (west) back onto the dirt road and return to the roadside Trials Area Trailhead parking lot at 5.1 miles.

MILES AND DIRECTIONS

0.0 Start from the northwest corner of the parking area and begin riding north up the dirt road.

0.5 Come to fence with a "San Ysidro Trials Area" sign.

1.2 Reach the main Trials Area parking lot and locate the trail behind the information kiosk.

1.6 At a fork in the trail, stay left (northeast) to continue on the Trials Area Trail.

2.0 Reach the canyon, dubbed the "Grand Canyon" by the bikers who come here. Turn right (south) to ride along the western side of the canyon.

2.5 The canyon becomes shallow and begins to open up as the trail drops down into the canyon.

2.6 The trail makes a right (southwest) turn out of the canyon.

San Ysidro Trials Area Trail

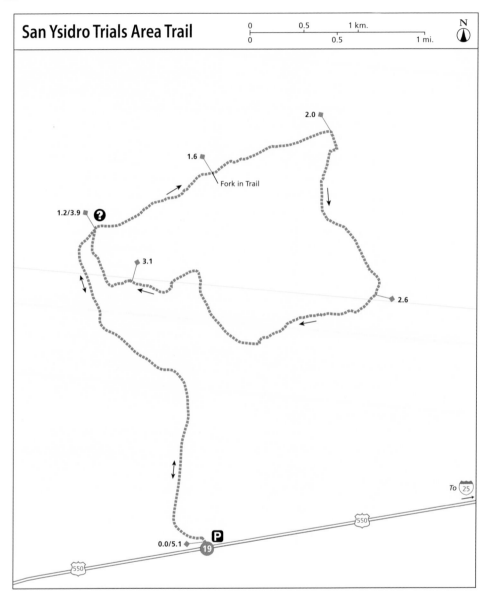

3.1 Cross a dry wash and continue riding northwest.

3.9 Return to the main Trials Area parking lot. Turn left (west), back onto the dirt road to return to the roadside parking area.

5.1 Arrive back at the roadside Trials Area Trailhead parking lot.

Local Attractions/Events

Jemez Springs Bath House, 062 Jemez Springs Plaza, Jemez Springs; (575) 829-3303; www.jemezsprings.org/bathhouse.html

Valles Caldera National Preserve, 18161 Hwy. 4, Jemez Springs; (505) 661-3333; www.vallescaldera.gov

Local Bike Shops

The Bike Coop, 120 Yale Blvd. SE, Albuquerque; (505) 265-5170; www.bike coop.com

The Bike Smith, 901 Rio Grande Blvd. NW, Albuquerque; (505) 242-9253; www.thebikesmith.com

Routes, Rentals, and Tours, 404 San Filipe St. NW, Albuquerque; (505) 933-5667; http://routesrentals.com

Trek Bicycle Superstore, 5000 Menaul Blvd. NE, Albuquerque; (505) 312-7243; www.trekbicyclesuperstore.com

Two Wheel Drive, 1706 Central Ave. SE, Albuquerque; (505) 243-8443; www .twowheeldrive.com

Restaurants

El Pinto Restaurant and Cantina, 10500 4th St. NW, Albuquerque; (505) 898-1771; www.elpinto.com

Frontier Restaurant, 2400 Central Ave. SE, Albuquerque; (505) 266-0550; www.frontierrestaurant.com

Taj Mahal, 1430 Carlisle Blvd. NE, Albuquerque; (505) 255-1994; www.taj mahalcuisineofindia.com

East Fork Trail:
Battleship Rock to Jemez Falls

The East Fork Trail is a wonderful riding destination in the Santa Fe National Forest. The section of the trail that runs from Battleship Rock to Jemez Springs is a popular destination for nature lovers. McCauley Hot Springs, located along the trail, provides visitors with a place to rest and relax midway between the start and end points.

Start: Battleship Rock parking area on the south side of NM 4

Length: 7.2 miles out and back

Riding time: 2 to 3 hours

Best bike: Mountain bike

Terrain and trail surface: Dirt-packed singletrack

Traffic and hazards: Motorized vehicles are not permitted on the trail. Riders may encounter hikers and equestrians.

Map: USGS Jemez Springs

Trail contacts: Santa Fe National Forest, PO Box 150, Jemez Springs 87025; (505) 829-3535; www.fs.fed.us/r3/sfe/districts/jemez/visitus.html

Special considerations: Trail may be snowy and icy in the winter. Poison ivy and water hemlock, a highly poisonous plant, are both present in this area.

Getting there: From Albuquerque, take I-25 North to exit 242 toward US 550/Bernalillo. Turn left (west) onto US 550 and drive north for 22.8 miles to the town of San Ysidro and the turn for NM 4. Turn right (northeast) onto NM 4 and continue 23.1 miles to the trailhead parking area, on the right (south). **GPS:** N35 49.700' / W106 38.647'

THE RIDE

The Battleship Rock to Jemez Falls section of the East Fork Trail (137) offers riders a challenging uphill climb with a rewarding view of 70-foot-tall Jemez Falls. The ride back is a much easier downhill journey, with the option to rest your legs in the McCauley Hot Springs, or warm springs as some people call them. Battleship Rock stands 200 feet tall. This interesting geologic feature

Jemez Falls

Battleship Rock and East Fork Jemez River

is made of compacted ash from volcanic eruptions that occurred millions of years ago.

The Battleship Rock Picnic Area is located just before the day-use parking area you have been directed to for this ride. (*Note:* There is a fee for parking in the picnic area.) Water is available at the picnic area, so be sure to fill up before you start your ride.

From the Battleship Rock parking area, locate the East Fork Trailhead just behind the pit toilets and begin riding south down through the picnic area and down to the East Fork of the Jemez River. The trail runs along the river for only a short distance before it begins to climb above and away from the river at 0.2 mile. The trail switchbacks a few times before it begins a long, steady ascent and then levels out at an ideal spot for a quick break or a snack at 1.1 miles.

Continue riding southeast through the mostly pine forest on the packed dirt trail. Come to another good rest area at 1.7 miles that offers large boulders to sit on just off the trail, so you won't be in the way of other riders and hikers. After riding another 0.8 mile, you reach the McCauley Hot Springs. The springs sit high above the East Fork, and there are several areas around the springs to sit and eat or rest. Many backpackers choose to camp overnight in this area.

Once you are finished with the hot springs, continue your ascent of the East Fork Trail. At 2.9 miles the East Fork Trail intersects an unnamed trail. Continue straight (southeast) on the East Fork Trail until you reach a spur trail at 3.3 miles. The spur trail to the right (south) leads to the Jemez Falls overlook. Turn right (south) to take this spur trail to the falls at 3.6 miles. Turn around here and return to the Battleship Rock parking area via the same route for a round-trip of 7.2 miles.

MILES AND DIRECTIONS

0.0 Start from the East Fork Trailhead, just behind the pit toilets, and begin riding south.

0.2 The trail begins to ascend away from the East Fork of the Jemez River.

1.1 Come to a good area to take a rest after a moderate ascent.

1.7 Reach an area that would make another good resting spot or a campsite, depending on your route.

2.5 Come to McCauley Hot Springs.

2.9 The trail intersects another unsigned trail. Continue straight (southeast).

3.3 Reach the Jemez Springs spur trail. Turn right (south) onto the spur trail to reach the falls.

3.6 Reach Jemez Falls. Turn around here and return via the same route.

7.2 Arrive back at Battleship Rock and the trailhead parking area.

East Fork Trail: Battleship Rock to Jemez Falls

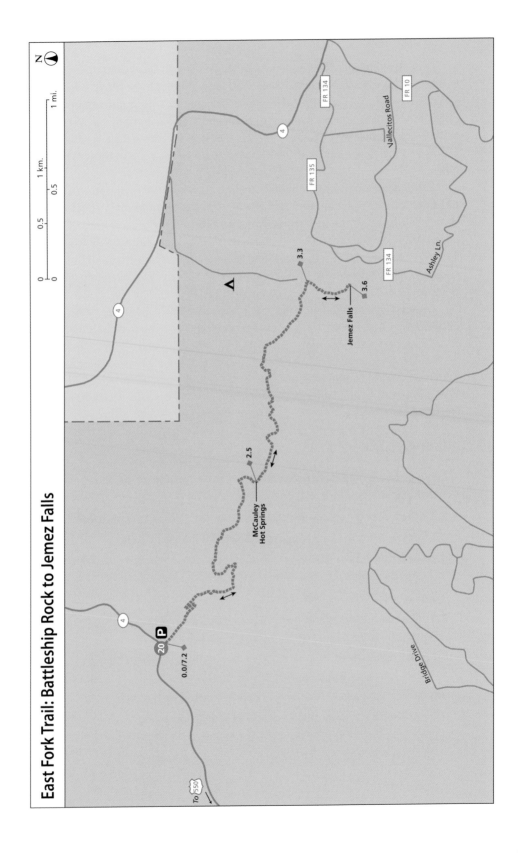

Local Attractions/Events

Jemez Springs Bath House, 062 Jemez Springs Plaza, Jemez Springs; (575) 829-3303; www.jemezsprings.org/bathhouse.html

Jemez State Monument and Heritage Area, PO Box 143, Jemez Springs; (575) 829-3530; www.nmmonuments.org/jemez

Local Bike Shops

Mellow Velo Bicycles, 132 E Marcy St., Santa Fe; (505) 995-8356; www.mellow velo.com

REI, 500 Markey St., Santa Fe; (505) 982-3557; www.rei.com

Sirius Cycles Bicycle Shop, 2801 Rodeo Rd., Santa Fe; (505) 819-7311; http://sirius-cycles.com

SpinDoc, 628 Old Las Vegas Hwy., Santa Fe; (505) 466-4181; www.spindoc.com

Restaurants

Bumble Bee's Baja Grill, 301 Jefferson St., Santa Fe; (505) 820-2862; www.bumblebeesbajagrill.com

Harry's Roadhouse, 96B Old Las Vegas Hwy., Santa Fe; (505) 989-4629; www.harrysroadhousesantafe.com

Jambo Cafe, 2010 Cerrillos Rd., Santa Fe; (505) 473-1269; http://jambocafe.net

The Shed, 113½ E Palace Ave., Santa Fe; (505) 982-9030; www.sfshed.com

East Fork Trail: East Fork Trailhead to Las Conchas Trailhead

The East Fork of the Jemez River originates in the Valles Caldera as a small meandering stream in a vast crater. The latter part of this trail follows the course of the East Fork. This portion of the river was designated as a National Wild and Scenic River in 1990.

Start: East Fork Trailhead, on the east side of NM 4

Length: 9.6 miles out and back

Riding time: 2 to 4 hours

Best bike: Mountain bike

Terrain and trail surface: Packed-dirt singletrack; forest road crossings; wooden footbridge crossings

Traffic and hazards: Motorized vehicles are not permitted on the trail. Riders may encounter hikers, backpackers, and equestrians.

Map: USGS Jemez Springs

Trail contacts: Santa Fe National Forest, PO Box 150, Jemez Springs 87025; (505) 829-3535; www.fs.fed.us/r3/sfe/districts/jemez/visitus.html

Special considerations: Trail may be snowy and icy in the winter. Poison ivy and water hemlock, a highly poisonous plant, are both present in this area.

Getting there: From Albuquerque, take I-25 North to exit 242 toward US 550/Bernalillo. Turn left (west) onto US 550 and drive north for 22.8 miles to the town of San Ysidro and the turn for NM 4. Turn right (northeast) onto NM 4 and continue 32.6 miles to the trailhead parking area, on the right (south). **GPS:** N35 49.185' / W106 35.423'

THE RIDE

The East Fork of the Jemez River passes through the heart of the Jemez Mountains' most popular recreation area on its way to its confluence with the Rio San Antonio. This trail takes you through a conifer forest, aspen groves, and wildflower meadows before dropping down to meander along the banks of this National Wild and Scenic River.

East Fork Trail near Las Conchas Trailhead

East Fork Trail: East Fork Trailhead to Las Conchas Trailhead

> 🍃 **Green Tip**
> *It may be cute to see a squirrel nibbling away at food other riders/campers left behind. But do you know the damage that can cause? Animals that become habituated to human food become a campground nuisance. Even more important, our food is not part of their natural diet and is therefore not good for them. Keep humans and animals safe by never feeding wildlife and by storing your food where wildlife cannot reach it.*

The trailhead is located on the northeast side of the parking area, just past the outhouse. A large Santa Fe National Forest sign greets users, and just beyond that the trail begins through the hiker's maze. There is a large interpretive map of the East Fork Trail here. The obvious dirt path leads east through a mostly pine forest. Several undesignated trails cross through the area, and the trail occasionally joins a rough forest road, which seems a bit confusing. Continue northeast on the main trail, occasionally marked with white triangles, and you'll be fine. At 0.4 mile the trail leaves the forest road on the left (northeast). As you continue, you begin to see aspen trees, and at 0.8 mile a spur trail joins from the right. Continue east on the main trail/forest road.

At 0.9 mile the East Fork Trail breaks off from the forest road once again. Look for the wooden trail sign marked "137." At 1.1 miles you come to the spur trail that provides access to the area known as "The Box." This term refers to the area being a box canyon—one that has walls on three sides. Continue right (east) on the East Fork Trail (#137) toward the Las Conchas Trailhead. At 1.4 miles the trail rejoins the forest road for about 0.1 mile before breaking off to the left (east). Cross the forest road again at 2.0 miles and continue southeast. The trail is singletrack through the aspens here. In spring and summer, look for wildflowers like Indian paintbrush. This is also a good area to spot butterflies in late spring; look for the striking yellow-and-black western tiger swallowtail.

The trail begins to descend the ridge to the valley below at 2.6 miles. During the warmer months, look for red-and-yellow shooting star columbine along the trail's rocky shoulder. Cross through a hikers maze at 3.0 miles and continue to descend the ridge into the canyon below.

At 3.2 miles you reach the East Fork of the Jemez River. This river is protected as a National Wild and Scenic River. At this point you have a great view of The Box if you look to the left (west). The trail continues east (right), following the flow of the river. At 3.3 miles cross the first of seven wooden footbridges that cross the river and muddy sections of the trail. This beautiful area is popular with anglers due to a healthy population of rainbow trout. Reach the Las Conchas Trailhead at 4.8 miles. Unless you have set up a shuttle, you will need to return to the East Fork Trailhead via the same route for a round-trip of 9.6 miles.

MILES AND DIRECTIONS

0.0 Start from the trailhead and ride east on the obvious dirt path.

0.4 The trail leaves the forest road; continue northeast.

0.8 Come to a spur trail; continue east on the main trail/forest road.

0.9 The East Fork Trail leaves the forest road; watch for a wooden trail sign marked "137."

1.1 Reach spur trail to The Box; continue right (east) on the East Fork Trail (#137) toward the Las Conchas Trailhead.

1.4 Return to forest road for about 0.1 mile; watch for the trail to break left (east).

2.0 Cross the forest road; continue southeast.

2.6 The trail descends the ridge.

3.0 Come to a hikers maze; continue to descend the ridge.

3.2 Reach the East Fork of the Jemez River; continue east (right).

3.3 Cross the first of seven wooden footbridges; continue east.

4.8 Reach the Las Conchas Trailhead; return to the East Fork Trailhead via the same route.

9.6 Arrive back at the East Fork Trailhead.

RIDE INFORMATION

Local Attractions/Events
Bandelier National Monument, 15 Entrance Rd., Los Alamos; (505) 672-3861, ext. 517; www.nps.gov/band/index.htm
Fenton Lake State Park, 455 Fenton Lake Rd., Jemez Springs; (575) 829-3630; www.emnrd.state.nm.us/SPD/fentonlakestatepark.html
Valles Caldera National Preserve, 39200 Hwy. 4, east of Jemez Springs; (505) 661-3333; www.vallescaldera.gov

East Fork Trail: East Fork Trailhead to Las Conchas Trailhead

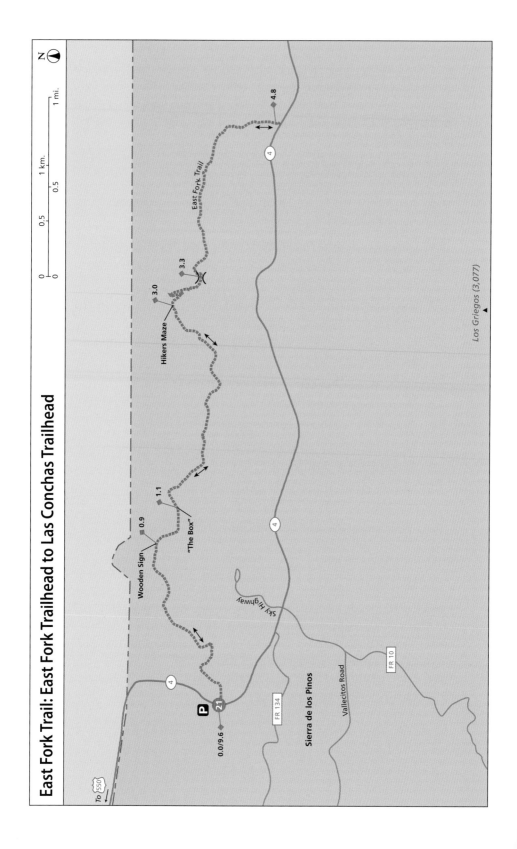

Local Bike Shops

The Broken Spoke, 1426 Cerrillos Rd., Santa Fe; (505) 992-3102; http://broken
spokesantafe.com

New Mexico Bike and Sport, 524 W Cordova Rd., Santa Fe; (505) 820-0809;
http://nmbikensport.com

Rob and Charlie's, 1632 St. Michaels Dr., Santa Fe; (505) 471-9119; www
.robandcharlies.com

Restaurants

Cafe Pasqual's, 121 Don Gaspar Ave., Santa Fe; (505) 983-9340; www.pasquals
.com

The Cowgirl, 319 S Guadalupe St., Santa Fe; (505) 982-2465; www.cowgirl
santafe.com

La Casa Sena La Cantina, 125 E Palace Ave., Santa Fe; (505) 988-9232; www
.lacasasena.com

Santa Fe Area

Valles Caldera National Preserve (Ride 22)

Santa Fe is one of the best biking cities in the Southwest. The city is easily commutable, and navigating through its streets is like navigating through history. As you cycle past the distinct Spanish-Pueblo architecture, enchanting cathedrals, and art museums, you realize just how unique and culturally diverse Santa Fe is. While in Santa Fe, take some time to visit the Santa Fe National Forest, located just minutes outside the city. Mountain bikers can be on the trail in minutes after leaving historic Santa Fe Plaza. Road bikers can head up Hyde Park Road and climb to the top of the Santa Fe ski area. Families can cruise along the Santa Fe Rail Trail for some scenic views. Additional outdoor recreation opportunities in Santa Fe include skiing in winter, rafting in summer, and hiking in fall. This historic and enchanting city really does have it all.

White Rock Visitor Center to Valles Caldera National Preserve

Offering gorgeous views of the Valles Caldera National Preserve, this challenging ride is a great option for exploring this unique area. The roadside parking areas in the preserve also offer excellent viewing opportunities of the elk that inhabit the caldera and regularly feed in the area nearby. Bring your binoculars!

Start: White Rock visitor center, in White Rock

Length: 49 miles out and back

Riding time: 5 to 8 hours

Best bike: Road bike

Terrain and trail surface: Paved road; gradual climb; a few descents outbound and mostly downhill on the return

Traffic and hazards: This is a highway, and riders should expect to encounter motorized vehicles. Shoulder space is limited on most of the ride.

Map: USGS Bland

Trail contacts: Valles Caldera National Preserve, 39200 Hwy. 4, Jemez Springs 87025; (505) 661-3333; www.vallescaldera.gov

Special considerations: Trail may be snowy and icy in the winter. Road may be closed after heavy snow.

Getting there: From Santa Fe, take US 285 North for 19 miles to the NM 502/Los Alamos exit. Continue on NM 502 for 11.8 miles and then merge left (south) onto NM 4. Continue for 4.6 miles to the White Rock visitor center, on your right (north). **GPS:** N35 49.644' / W106 12.713'

THE RIDE

This ride offers a little bit of everything: views of Santa Fe to the east, access to Bandelier National Monument, and sweeping views of the Valles Caldera National Preserve valley to the north. The largest extinct volcano in the world, Valles Caldera, also known as the Baca Ranch, is truly one of a kind.

The area is a 12-mile-wide collapsed volcanic crater, or caldera, formed when the earth collapsed after a catastrophic volcanic eruption took place

Jemez Mountains

A Good Rule of Thumb

Approaching wildlife is NEVER a good idea. A good rule of thumb is that if the wildlife you are viewing changes its behavior in any way, you are or are getting too close.

A fun way to teach children this rule is by actually using their thumbs. Have kids hold a thumb an arm's distance in front of their face. If their thumbnail doesn't "cover up" the animal they are looking at, they are probably too close and need to back up.

It's not an exact science, but it will help kids learn to slow down and think about how close they actually are to wild animals.

here some 1.2 million years ago. The scenery here is striking, with high-altitude grasslands, meadows lush with wildflowers, conifer forests and woodlands, hot springs, crystal-clear rivers and streams, and high-mountain domes. The area is home to nearly 8,000 elk, the largest elk herd in state, and also contains many miles of pristine trout streams, thousands of acres of conifer forests, and several species of endangered plants and animals.

In July 2000, 140 square miles of the area was purchased to protect the historic Baca Ranch, resulting in the creation of the Valles Caldera National Preserve.

From the White Rock visitor center and parking area, turn left onto NM 4 and begin riding southwest. At 0.6 mile continue straight (southwest) through the intersection as the road heads out of town. The two-lane road is narrow and offers minimal shoulder space. This is a popular ride, though, and drivers tend to be quite cautious of riders. After leaving the city, the road begins a gradual descent into a large canyon and eventually reaches a steep descent just before arriving at the canyon floor at 5.3 miles. After snaking along the canyon floor, the road then climbs back up and out of the canyon along a narrow route that eventually emerges on top of a long ridge heading northwest.

At 7.6 miles you pass a boundary sign for Bandelier National Monument on the right (north) and then pass the park entrance on the left (south) at 8.1 miles. Views of the mountains to the east are uninterrupted along this section of the ride, and the hidden Frijoles Canyon is just a stone's throw away to the west. Continue riding northwest along NM 4; pass the Ponderosa Campground at 13.9 miles on the left (south) and then stay left (west) at 14 miles when you reach the intersection with NM 501. The steepest climbing begins just after this intersection, including a few very tight switchbacks.

As the road climbs higher into the mountains, you enter a pine forest. As the road levels out at 20 miles, you pass the Cerro Grande Trailhead and parking area on the right (north). The road then begins dropping down into the caldera and passes the Coyote Call Trail on the left (south) at 22.8 miles, just before arriving at the preserve's main entrance, on the right (west), at 24.5 miles. Turn around and return to the White Rock visitor center for a round-trip of 49 miles.

MILES AND DIRECTIONS

0.0 Start from the visitor center, turn right, and begin riding southwest on NM 4.

0.6 Continue straight (southwest) through the intersection.

5.3 A steep descent ends and a climb begins.

7.6 Pass a Bandelier National Monument park boundary sign.

8.1 Pass the entrance to Bandelier National Monument, on the left (south).

13.9 Ride past the Ponderosa Campground, on the left (south).

14.0 Stay left (west) on NM 4 at the intersection with NM 501.

20.0 Pass the Cero Grande parking area and trail, on the right (north).

22.8 Continue riding past the Coyote Call Trailhead, on the left (south).

24.5 Reach the main entrance for the Valles Caldera National Preserve, on the right (west). Return the way you came.

49.0 Arrive back at the White Rock visitor center parking area.

RIDE INFORMATION

Local Attraction
Fenton Lake State Park, 455 Fenton Lake Rd., Jemez Springs; (575) 829-3630; www.emnrd.state.nm.us/SPD/fentonlakestatepark.html

Local Bike Shops
Mellow Velo Bicycles, 132 E Marcy St., Santa Fe; (505) 995-8356; www.mellow velo.com
REI, 500 Markey St., Santa Fe; (505) 982-3557; www.rei.com
Sirius Cycles Bicycle Shop, 2801 Rodeo Rd., Santa Fe; (505) 819-7311; http://sirius-cycles.com
SpinDoc, 628 Old Las Vegas Hwy., Santa Fe; (505) 466-4181; www.spindoc.com

White Rock Visitor Center to Valles Caldera National Preserve

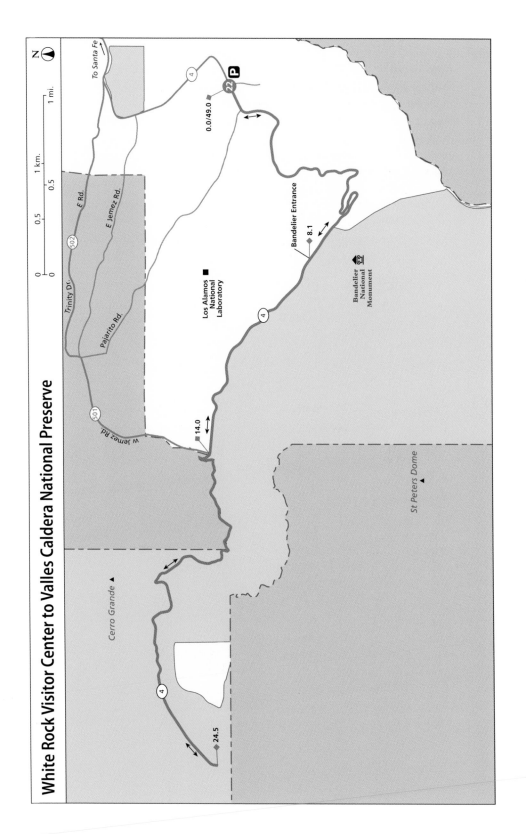

Restaurants

Bumble Bee's Baja Grill, 301 Jefferson St., Santa Fe; (505) 820-2862; www
.bumblebeesbajagrill.com

Harry's Roadhouse, 96B Old Las Vegas Hwy., Santa Fe; (505) 989-4629; www
.harrysroadhousesantafe.com

Jambo Cafe, 2010 Cerrillos Rd., Santa Fe; (505) 473-1269; www.jambocafe.net

The Shed, 113½ E Palace Ave., Santa Fe; (505) 982-9030; www.sfshed.com

Caja del Rio Trail

The Caja del Rio Trail is a fun and easily accessible trail for those who are new to mountain biking. The trail is also great for riders looking to gain some extra mileage under their pedals. The trail winds past livestock corrals and piñon trees and glides under the open New Mexico sky. Mostly flat with a few small gradual climbs, wide trails, and little obstacles, the Caja del Rio Trail will be enjoyable for the entire family.

Start: Small gravel pullout at the beginning of CR 62

Length: 15 miles out and back

Riding time: 2.5 to 3 hours

Best bike: Mountain bike

Terrain and trail surface: Doubletrack forest road; mostly smooth, with occasional uneven surfaces and gradual climbs

Traffic and hazards: Expect to encounter occasional motor vehicle traffic and cattle grazing throughout the trail.

Map: USGS Santa Fe County

Trail contacts: Santa Fe National Forest Headquarters, 11 Forest Ln., Santa Fe 87508; (505) 438-5300; www.fs.usda.gov/santafe

Special considerations: Caja del Rio Road can become muddy and impassable in wet conditions.

Getting there: From Santa Fe, drive north on St. Francis Road to US 84 North to NM 599. Follow NM 599 South for 7 miles and turn right onto exit 6. Veer right and take the roundabout to Caja del Rio Road. Drive for 1 mile and turn right to stay on Caja del Rio. Continue for 2.8 miles and turn left onto CR 62. There is a small gravel pullout on the right; the trail begins here. **GPS:** N35 41.113' / W106 04.348'

THE RIDE

"Caja del Rio" translates to "box of the river." This plateau encompasses over 80,000 acres just 15 minutes from downtown Santa Fe and stretches all the way to the Rio Grande. Many roads converge along FR 24, and the opportunities abound to create your own route. Caja del Rio is a volcanic field that includes cinder cones and basalt outflows. This area makes for a unique cycling experience.

Blue skies and dirt roads last for days in Santa Fe.

The trail begins on a compacted, smooth doubletrack county road. At 0.9 mile the trail passes the Caja del Rio Landfill, to the left of the trail. Not a pleasing sight, but it puts the amount of waste we create into perspective. Soon after passing the landfill at 1.1 miles, CR 62 intersects FR 24. Continue straight on FR 24 as the trail passes many private side roads. This part of the trail is fairly well maintained and may even be covered in gravel. As the trail glides pass piñon trees in this volcanic plateau, enjoy the views of the Sangre de Cristo Mountains.

At 2.1 miles the trail arrives at a cattleguard; there is a small unmarked road on the right. Continue straight across the cattleguard and continue on FR 24. The trail rolls gently up and down hills for this section. Continue straight across a second cattleguard at 2.4 miles. Begin a small descent, followed by a moderate climb. The trail slowly begins to reach the saddle of the plateau, and large open views make the trail feel desolate. Reach a split in the road at 3.9 miles; keep left as another trail angles in from the right.

The trail flattens out even more and allows for easier pedaling at 4.3 miles. Keep an eye out for dry and uneven trail surfaces—small and large dips have been formed from motor vehicle traffic in wet conditions. At 6.9 miles the trail crosses a third and final cattleguard; a small livestock corral is located to the right of the trail. Stay straight after crossing the cattleguard, and keep on the lookout for a road on the right with a small cattleguard crossing. This is your turnaround point. Take a much deserved break and enjoy the peaceful views and solitude found on this trail. Retrace the route back to the trailhead for a round-trip of 15 miles.

MILES AND DIRECTIONS

0.0 Start at a small gravel pullout on right at the beginning of CR 62.

0.9 The trail passes the Caja del Rio Landfill, on the left.

1.1 At the intersection with FR 24, take FR 24.

2.1 Pass an unmarked road on the right; continue straight on the trail and cross a cattleguard.

2.4 The trail crosses a second cattleguard and continues straight.

3.9 Keep left as another trail splits off to the right.

6.9 Remain straight as the trail crosses a third cattleguard and passes a small livestock corral on the right.

7.5 The trail reaches an open area with expansive views all around. The unmarked road on the right with a cattleguard is your turnaround point. Retrace the route back to the trailhead.

15.0 Arrive back at the small pullout and trailhead.

Caja del Rio Trail

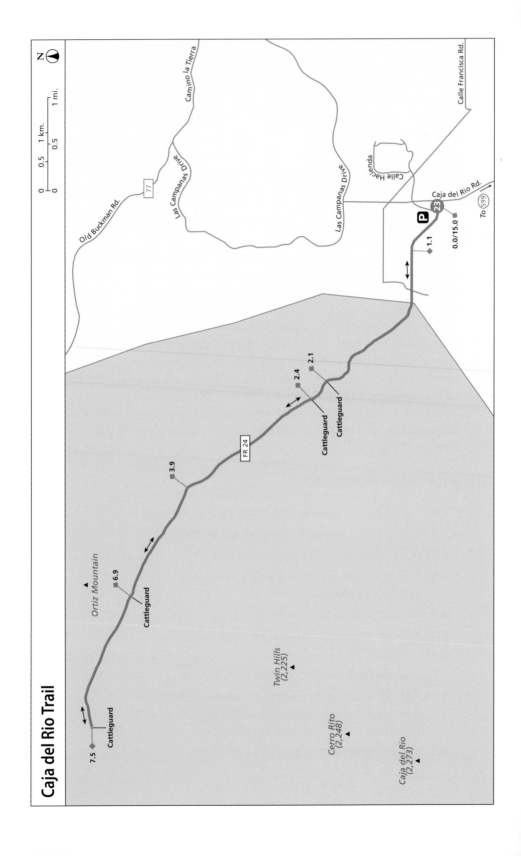

Local Attractions
Georgia O'Keeffe Museum, 217 Johnson St., Santa Fe; (505) 946-1000; www .okeeffemuseum.org
Museum of International Folk Art, 706 Camino Lejo, Santa Fe; (505) 476-1200; www.internationalfolkart.org

Local Bike Shops
The Broken Spoke, 1426 Cerrillos Rd., Santa Fe; (505) 992-3102; http://broken spokesantafe.com
New Mexico Bike and Sport, 524 W Cordova Rd., Santa Fe; (505) 820-0809; http://nmbikensport.com
Rob and Charlie's, 1632 St. Michaels Dr., Santa Fe; (505) 471-9119; www .robandcharlies.com

Restaurants
Cafe Pasqual's, 121 Don Gaspar Ave., Santa Fe; (505) 983-9340; www.pasquals .com
The Cowgirl, 319 S Guadalupe St., Santa Fe; (505) 982-2465; www.cowgirl santafe.com
La Casa Sena La Cantina, 125 E Palace Ave., Santa Fe; (505) 988-9232; www .lacasasena.com

Rio En Medio

"Rio En Medio" translates to "river in the middle," and that's exactly what you will find biking along this refreshing trail. Water cascades alongside the trailhead at Aspen Basin and all the way to the end of this out-and-back trail at Aspen Ranch. The Rio En Medio is a great trail if you're looking to find solitude from the crowds of Santa Fe. There are many shallow pools to cool off in, and plenty of plant and animal life may be found all along this unique trail.

Start: To the right of the information board at the Aspen Basin Trailhead parking area

Length: 4.8 miles out and back

Riding time: 2.5 hours

Best bike: Mountain bike

Terrain and trail surface: Mostly rocky singletrack with the occasional tree root; smooth singletrack on some sections

Traffic and hazards: Traffic is slower here than at other trails in the Santa Fe National Forest. Some downhill sections are loose and rocky. Trails can also be wet from the cascading waters.

Map: Dharma Maps, Santa Fe Explorer, 2012

Trail contacts: Santa Fe National Forest, 1474 Rodeo Rd., Santa Fe 87501; (505) 438-7840; www.fs.usda.gov/santafe/

Special considerations: Restrooms and a small camping area located at the trailhead and parking area.

Getting there: From Santa Fe, take St. Francis Drive and turn right onto Paseo de Peralta. Drive 1.5 miles and turn right onto Bishop Lodge Road. Continue 0.1 mile and turn right onto Artist Road, which becomes Hyde Park Road (NM 475). Continue straight for 16 miles to the Rio En Medio Trailhead parking area, on the left. **GPS:** N35 47.741' / W105 48.296'

THE RIDE

From the Aspen Basin Trailhead, the Rio En Medio is a constant descent for most of its length to Aspen Ranch, so your return ride will be mostly uphill. But with the coolness of the water and shade of the trees, the ascent is a pleasant one.

From the Aspen Basin parking area, locate the marker for the Winsor National Recreation Trail (#254), to the right of the restrooms and the trailhead

Roots and rocks are scattered along the length of the trail.

information board. Go right for 0.1 mile and cross the creek on a small bridge to arrive at the Rio En Medio (Trail #163), on your left. This is your route.

The trail is smooth at first and curves around until you reach 0.3 mile. The trail begins to run alongside the creek as it descends over an unforgiving technical and rocky terrain. Please use caution on this section; you may even need to walk down this on certain occasions. The trail remains this way until you reach 0.5 mile, where you enter a large grassy open meadow filled with beautiful aspen trees.

After you have exited the aspen meadow, remain straight along the trail as you continue to follow the creek. The trail descends into a damp, almost eerie, grove of trees that includes willow and Gambel oak, to name a few. Wildlife abounds, and plenty of birds, rabbits, and butterflies roam this area.

As you descend, keep an eye out for a trail on your left at 1.8 miles. This one may sneak past you, because it is not well marked and crosses the creek. If you do miss this trail, you will soon find out. In 0.2 mile you will pass a small meadow that has been used regularly as a campsite, and immediately after this you will reach a private fence boundary. If you reach this fence, turn around and retrace your route to the missed trail.

Once you have found the trail, cross the creek. After a small flat section, the trail begins to ascend a small hill. At 2.0 miles you cross a small drainage. After the drainage, the trail ascends to the right, reaching a national forest gate at 2.2 miles. Go straight through the gate and stay straight on the trail.

At 2.3 miles the trail crosses one last stream. After this crossing, stay left on the trail, arriving at the Aspen Ranch Trailhead at 2.4 miles. This trailhead also converges onto FR 412. If you didn't want to ride back to Aspen Basin for a full out-and-back, FR 412 connects to FR 102 and is accessible from Hyde Park Road (NM 475).

To return to the Aspen Basin Trailhead, retrace your route. Keep in mind that most of the trail will now be uphill. Take your time as you ascend the Rio En Medio, and enjoy the beauty of this great trail from a different perspective for a round-trip of 4.8 miles.

MILES AND DIRECTIONS

0.0 Start at the Aspen Basin Trailhead to the Winsor National Recreation Trail (#254), located to the right of the restrooms and information board.

0.1 After crossing a small bridge, turn left onto the Rio En Medio (Trail #163).

Rio En Medio

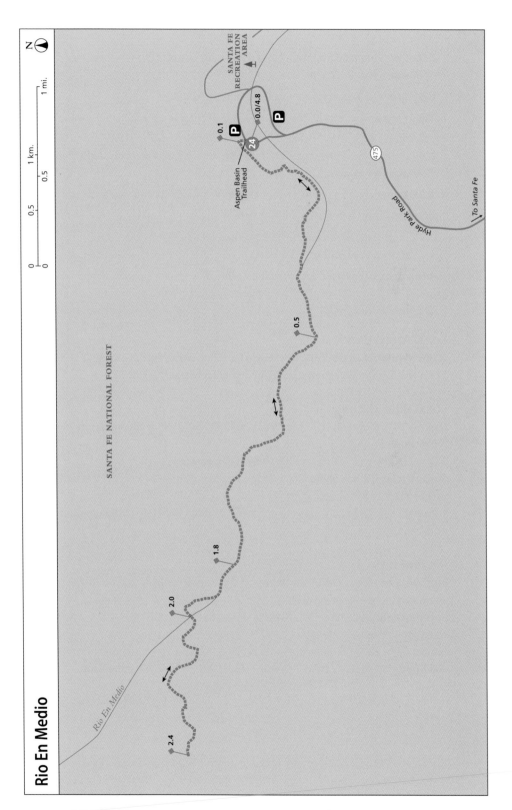

N

0   0.5   1 km.

0   0.5   1 mi.

SANTA FE NATIONAL FOREST

Rio En Medio

2.4

2.0

1.8

0.5

Aspen Basin
Trailhead

0.1

P

0.0/4.8

P

24

SANTA FE
RECREATION
AREA

475

Hyde Park Road

To Santa Fe

0.3 Continue straight on Trail 163 down very steep, rocky terrain alongside a flowing creek.

0.5 Arrive at a grassy opening. Continue straight.

1.8 Keep an eye out for the trail on left that crosses over the creek. (**Note:** If you miss this turn, you will reach a private fence in 0.2 mile.)

2.0 Cross a small drainage. The trail is on the right and ascends slightly after the crossing.

2.2 Pass through a wooden gate. Continue straight as you descend.

2.3 Cross one last stream and stay left.

2.4 Reach the Aspen Ranch Trailhead and FR 412. Turn around and retrace your route.

4.8 Arrive back at the Aspen Basin Trailhead.

RIDE INFORMATION

Local Attraction
Hyde Memorial State Park, 740 Hyde Park Rd., Santa Fe 87501; (505) 983-7175; www.emnrd.state.nm.us/SPD/hydememorialstatepark.html

Local Bike Shops
Mellow Velo Bicycles, 132 E Marcy St., Santa Fe; (505) 995-8356; www.mellowvelo.com
REI, 500 Markey St., Santa Fe; (505) 982-3557; www.rei.com
Sirius Cycles Bicycle Shop, 2801 Rodeo Rd., Santa Fe; (505) 819-7311; http://sirius-cycles.com
SpinDoc, 628 Old Las Vegas Hwy., Santa Fe; (505) 466-4181; www.spindoc.com

Restaurants
Bumble Bee's Baja Grill, 301 Jefferson St., Santa Fe, NM; (505) 820-2862; www.bumblebeesbajagrill.com
Harry's Roadhouse, 96B Old Las Vegas Hwy., Santa Fe; (505) 989-4629; www.harrysroadhousesantafe.com
Jambo Cafe, 2010 Cerrillos Rd., Santa Fe; (505) 473-1269; www.jambocafe.net
The Shed, 113½ E Palace Ave., Santa Fe; (505) 982-9030; www.sfshed.com

Borrego, Winsor National Recreation, and Bear Wallow Trails Loop

The Borrego, Winsor, and Bear Wallow Trails Loop just may be one of the most popular trails along Hyde Park Road. Perhaps that's because of its close proximity to Hyde Memorial State Park. Many locals flock here after work for a quick bike ride or jog with their dog for a super fun loop. Bring a friend and cool off in one of the creeks during the hot and dry summer months.

Start: Borrego Trailhead parking area

Length: 4.1-mile lollipop loop

Riding time: 1.5 hours

Best bike: Mountain bike

Terrain and trail surface: Good climbs and descents on a smooth singletrack; some rocky areas

Traffic and hazards: The trail is heavily used by other cyclists, trail runners, and day hikers.

Map: Dharma Maps, Santa Fe Explorer, 2012

Trail contacts: Santa Fe National Forest Headquarters, 11 Forest Ln., Santa Fe 87508; (505) 438-5300; www.fs.usda.gov/santafe

Special considerations: Leashed dogs are allowed on these trails.

Getting there: From Santa Fe, take St. Francis Drive and turn right onto Paseo de Peralta. Drive 1.5 miles and turn right onto Bishop Lodge Road. Go 0.1 mile and turn right onto Artist Road, which becomes Hyde Park Road (NM 475). Continue straight for 8.5 miles to the Borrego Trailhead parking area, on the left. **GPS:** N35 44.777' / W105 50.063'

THE RIDE

The Borrego, Winsor, and Bear Wallow Triangle is a moderate trail with only about 800 feet of elevation gain. This is a great trail for the whole entire family. Even the pooch can come play on these dog-friendly trails. The loop can be ridden from either direction, but most people prefer doing the Bear Wallow Trail at the end. Escape to the shade of the trees in summer and enjoy every wonderful thing nature has to offer you here on the Borrego, Winsor National

The Borrego Trail glides as it parallels the creek.

Recreation, and Bear Wallow Trails. Pack a lunch and take off from work early to enjoy this great trail.

Beginning at the Borrego Trailhead and parking area, locate the Borrego Trailhead sign "#150." The trail begins at the bottom of the steps and veers to the right. The first 0.5 mile is a smooth and wide rolling downhill. At 0.4 mile keep right at the split on the Borrego Trail. The trail begins a gradual climb. Then, at 0.8 mile, there is a nice sweeping downhill that eventually levels out and rolls alongside Tesuque Creek. A small unmarked trail on the left leads to the creek at 1.5 miles. Continue straight on Borrego.

At 1.6 miles a small wooden bridge carries the trail over Tesuque Creek. Keep straight and continue through the field to the Winsor Trail. Reach the Winsor Trail (#254) at 1.7 miles and turn left. The trail begins another descent; take your time—the trail is a bit loose and rocky underfoot. Keep an eye out for the Bear Wallow Trail (#182) on the left side of the creek at 2.5 miles. Bear Wallow crosses a small wooden bridge and immediately veers right uphill, followed by a series of steep switchbacks. Continue on Bear Wallow until it returns to the Borrego Trail at 3.7 miles; turn right. At 4.1 miles, after a moderate climb, arrive back at the Borrego Trailhead and parking area.

MILES AND DIRECTIONS

0.0 Start from the parking area and locate the Borrego Trailhead, signed "#150." The trail begins down the step and veers to the right.

0.4 Keep right at split and continue on the Borrego Trail (#150).

1.5 An unmarked trail on the left leads to the river; keep straight.

1.6 The trail crosses Tesuque Creek on a small wooden bridge; continue straight through the field.

1.7 Arrive at the Winsor Trail (#254); turn left.

2.5 Turn left onto the Bear Wallow Trail (#182) as it crosses a bridge over Tesuque Creek.

3.7 Return to the Borrego Trail; keep right.

4.1 Arrive back at the Borrego Trailhead parking area.

RIDE INFORMATION

Local Bike Shops
The Broken Spoke, 1426 Cerrillos Rd., Santa Fe; (505) 992-3102; http://broken spokesantafe.com

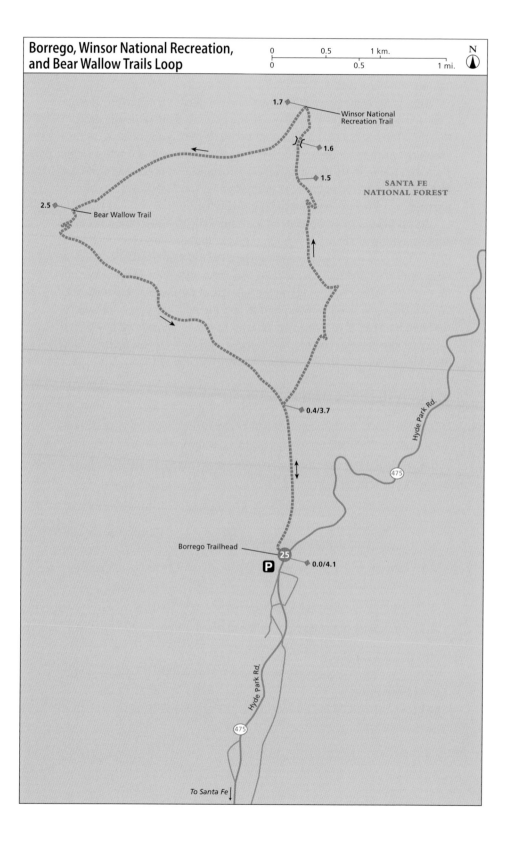

Borrego, Winsor National Recreation, and Bear Wallow Trails Loop

0   0.5   1 km.

0   0.5   1 mi.

N

1.7

Winsor National
Recreation Trail

1.6

1.5

SANTA FE
NATIONAL FOREST

2.5

Bear Wallow Trail

Hyde Park Rd.

475

0.4/3.7

Borrego Trailhead

25

P

0.0/4.1

Hyde Park Rd.

475

To Santa Fe

New Mexico Bike and Sport, 524 W Cordova Rd., Santa Fe; (505) 820-0809; http://nmbikensport.com

Rob and Charlie's, 1632 St. Michaels Dr., Santa Fe; (505) 471-9119; www.robandcharlies.com

Restaurants

Cafe Pasqual's, 121 Don Gaspar Ave., Santa Fe; (505) 983-9340; www.pasquals.com

The Cowgirl, 319 S Guadalupe St., Santa Fe; (505) 982-2465; www.cowgirlsantafe.com

La Casa Sena La Cantina, 125 E Palace Ave., Santa Fe; (505) 988-9232; www.lacasasena.com

Aspen Vista Trail

Aspen Vista is a great endurance ride with a constant but gradual gain in elevation until you reach the summit of Tesuque Peak at 12,040 feet. The trail contours along the Sangre De Cristo Mountain Range. As the trail climbs it passes through aspen-covered forests, crosses small rushing creeks, and offers expansive views around every corner. The best time of year to ride this trail is during fall, when the turning foliage paints the views in majestic hues of orange and yellow. Fall is also the busiest time of year on the Aspen Vista Trail, but it is wide and can easily accommodate a large crowd.

Start: Aspen Vista Picnic Area

Length: 12 miles out and back

Riding time: 3.5 hours

Best bike: Mountain bike

Terrain and trail surface: National forest road and well-packed doubletrack trails

Traffic and hazards: Expect to encounter many other cyclists, trail runners, and day hikers. The gate at the trailhead remains locked, and the trail may only be accessed by motor vehicles with permits.

Map: Dharma Maps, Santa Fe Explorer, 2012

Trail contacts: Santa Fe National Forest, 1474 Rodeo Rd., Santa Fe 87505; (505) 438-7840; www.fs.usda.gov/santafe

Special considerations: There may be snow on Tesuque Peak as late as June. Restrooms and a picnic area are located at the Aspen Vista Trailhead. The trail reaches 12,040 feet; take the time to adjust if visiting from areas of lower elevation.

Getting there: From Santa Fe, take St. Francis Drive and turn right onto Paseo de Peralta. Drive 1.5 miles and turn right onto Bishop Lodge Road.

Go 0.1 mile and turn right onto Artist Road, which becomes Hyde Park Road (NM 475). Continue straight for 13 miles to the Aspen Vista Picnic Area, on the right. **GPS:** N35 46.636' / W105 48.646'

THE RIDE

The Aspen Vista Trail is a super fun and rewarding trail. The trail is great for cyclists looking to summit a peak, but on a gradual gradient. The reward is Tesuque Peak, rising to 12,040 feet. Though the peak itself is home to an electronic site, the views and alpine tundra environment found at the summit overshadow the electronics. Be aware that the trail may still have snow debris as late as June as it nears the summit.

From the Aspen Vista Picnic Area, locate the trailhead next to the information board. The Aspen Vista Trail is also known as FR 150. Ride past the

One of the many viewpoints from the summit

large gate and the trail opens up to a dirt road. At this point you're at around 10,000 feet of elevation. The trail is somewhat dense for the first 0.5 mile and gradually opens up to views on the right. At 0.8 mile the trail passes over the refreshing Tesuque Creek; the Tesuque Trail is on the right. The trail begins to climb steadily, preparing your lungs and legs for the push ahead.

At 1.5 miles a large rock outcrop on the right provides views as well as a nice place to take a breather and drink some water. At around 2.0 miles the trail begins to climb more steeply. The trail rounds a corner to the right at 2.5 miles and stretches straight on as trees line both sides of the trail on this small but continuous gradient. At the end of this section, the trail curves sharply to the left and climbs up until, at mile 3.9, you arrive at a small meadow that is a great place to turn around if you are not looking to reach the summit. If you walk out into the meadow on the left, the views are astounding and offer a glimpse of the trail below.

Continuing from the meadow, the trail cuts back to the right and gradually climbs for about 0.5 mile through a dense tree-lined area. Soon these dense woods open up on the left and the trail is getting close to the summit. At 5.4 miles the trail enters a large alpine meadow. Continue straight and pass three large wooden fences. The trail passes under the Tesuque ski lift at 5.6 miles and continues straight. At 5.8 miles the trail curves to the right. Stay to the right once you have reached the Ski Patrol and follow the trail up the hill to electronic site.

The Aspen Vista Trail reaches the summit of Tesuque Peak at 6.0 miles. You won't be disappointed. From Penitente Peak to Santa Fe Lake, the views are expansive from every angle. Once you have enjoyed the summit, take your time as you begin the long descent back to the picnic area for a round-trip of 12.0 miles.

MILES AND DIRECTIONS

0.0 Start at the Aspen Vista Trailhead/FR 150, next to the picnic area information board. Ride through the gate and continue straight.

0.8 Pass the Tesuque Trail, on the right.

1.5 A large rock outcrop on the right provides a great viewpoint and rest spot.

3.9 Arrive at a small meadow on the left; the trail cuts back to the right.

5.4 The trail enters a large alpine meadow; continue straight and pass through three fences.

5.6 Pass under the Tesuque ski lift.

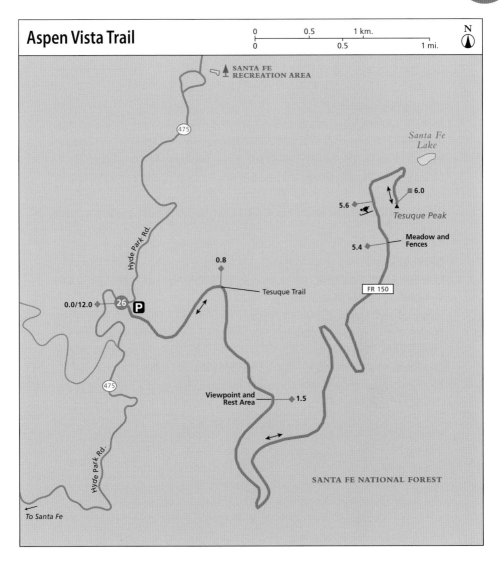

Aspen Vista Trail

| | 0 | 0.5 | 1 km. |
| 0 | | 0.5 | 1 mi. |

N

SANTA FE
RECREATION AREA

475

*Santa Fe
Lake*

6.0

5.6

Tesuque Peak

5.4 — Meadow and
Fences

0.8

Tesuque Trail

FR 150

0.0/12.0 — 26 — P

Hyde Park Rd.

475

Viewpoint and
Rest Area — 1.5

SANTA FE NATIONAL FOREST

Hyde park Rd.

To Santa Fe

5.8 The trail curves to the right. Veer right once you have reached the Ski
Patrol and follow the trail up the hill to the electronic site.

6.0 Reach Tesuque Peak. Turn around and retrace your route back down
to the trailhead.

12.0 Arrive back at the Aspen Vista Trailhead.

RIDE INFORMATION

Local Attraction

Ski Santa Fe New Mexico, 1477 Hwy. 475, Santa Fe 87501; (505) 988-9636; http://skisantafe.com

Local Bike Shops

Mellow Velo Bicycles, 132 E Marcy St., Santa Fe; (505) 995-8356; www.mellow velo.com

REI, 500 Markey St., Santa Fe; (505) 982-3557; www.rei.com

Sirius Cycles Bicycle Shop, 2801 Rodeo Rd., Santa Fe; (505) 819-7311; http://sirius-cycles.com

SpinDoc, 628 Old Las Vegas Hwy., Santa Fe; (505) 819-7311; www.spindoc .com

Restaurants

Bumble Bee's Baja Grill, 301 Jefferson St., Santa Fe; (505) 820-2862; www .bumblebeesbajagrill.com

Harry's Roadhouse, 96B Old Las Vegas Hwy., Santa Fe; (505) 989-4629; www .harrysroadhousesantafe.com

Jambo Cafe, 2010 Cerrillos Rd., Santa Fe; (505) 473-1269; www.jambocafe.net

The Shed, 113½ E Palace Ave., Santa Fe; (505) 982-9030; www.sfshed.com

Aspen Ranch Trail

The Aspen Ranch out-and-back, combines FR 102 and FR 412 to create a great trail for the beginner mountain biker. The route stretches for almost 9 miles, and you may find unexpected solitude within its boundaries. Most traffic will be other cyclists, but there will be the occasional motor vehicle. The trails are wide and offer optimal room for playing around.

Start: Small gravel parking lot just above the beginning of FR 102, on left side of Hyde Park Road (NM 475)

Length: 8.8 miles out and back.

Riding time: 2.5 hours

Best bike: Mountain bike

Terrain and trail surface: Smooth forest roads that provide a wide, open trail

Traffic and hazards: Aspen Ranch combines FR 102 and FR 412. Expect to encounter motor vehicle traffic, trail runners, hikers, and other cyclists.

Map: Dharma Maps, Santa Fe Explorer, 2012.

Trail contacts: Santa Fe National Forest Headquarters, 11 Forest Ln., Santa Fe 87508; (505) 438-5300; www.fs.usda.gov/santafe

Special considerations: Leashed dogs are allowed on the trails. The roads can become impassable when wet.

Getting there: From Santa Fe, take St. Francis Drive and turn right onto Paseo de Peralta. Drive 1.5 miles and turn right onto Bishop Lodge Road. Go 0.1 mile and turn right onto Artist Road, which becomes Hyde Park Road (NM 475). Continue straight for 12.5 miles to the FR 102 parking area on the left, just above FR 102. **GPS:** N35 46.409' / W105 48.663'

THE RIDE

Aspen Ranch is great for those looking to take out their new gravel grinders. Smooth, wide-open forest roads provide a smooth, yet challenging at times trail. This route is supposedly great to travel during a full moon, when the trail can be very visible at night. Sunsets are great to watch from certain portions of the trail as well. The route itself isn't too congested with traffic; even on weekends, the route remains pretty quiet to motorized vehicles.

Beginning at the gravel parking area, make a slight right onto Hyde Park Road (NM 475) and then an immediate right onto FR 102. The trail weaves along the edge of the Sangre de Cristo Mountains and passes the Winsor National Recreation Trail on both sides of FR 102 at 2.0 miles. The trail is a constant downhill until it reaches an intersection at 3.0 miles. Turn right at the intersection onto FR 412. The trail makes an almost immediate left at 3.1 miles and begins its first climb. On the ascent, keep right as FR 412 passes the trail to Aspen Cabin, to the left of the trail.

Trees provide ample shade on Aspen Ranch.

Reach an open meadow filled with sprawling aspens lining both sides of the trail at 4.0 miles. The trail flattens out for a bit and continues straight. After a gradual uphill, reach a small gravel parking area on the right at 4.4 miles. This marks the Aspen Ranch Trailhead and the turnaround point for this ride. Retrace the route back to the parking area for a round-trip of 8.8 miles. Remember that the ride back will be more climbing than at the beginning. But it is a moderate climb of 900 feet stretched over 4.4 miles.

MILES AND DIRECTIONS

0.0 Start at the gravel parking area. Make a slight right onto Hyde Park Road (NM 475) and then an immediate right onto FR 102.

2.0 Pass the Winsor National Recreation Trail, on both sides of FR 102.

3.0 Arrive at a three-way intersection. Turn right onto FR 412.

3.1 FR 412 makes a sharp left turn and begins to climb.

3.6 Keep right on FR 412 as the trail passes the trail to Aspen Cabin, on the left.

4.0 The trail opens to a meadow filled with aspen trees.

4.4 A small gravel parking lot on the right welcomes you to the Aspen Ranch Trailhead. Turn around and retrace the route back to the parking area.

8.8 Arrive back at the parking area off Hyde Park Road.

RIDE INFORMATION

Local Attraction
San Miguel Mission, 401 Old Santa Fe Trail, Santa Fe 87501; (505) 983-3974; http://santafe.org/Visiting_Santa_Fe/Entertainment/Historic_Sites

Local Bike Shops
The Broken Spoke, 1426 Cerrillos Road, Santa Fe; (505) 992-3102; http://brokenspokesantafe.com

New Mexico Bike and Sport, 524 W Cordova Road, Santa Fe; (505) 820-0809; http://nmbikensport.com

Rob and Charlie's, 1632 St. Michaels Dr., Santa Fe; (505) 471-9119; www.robandcharlies.com

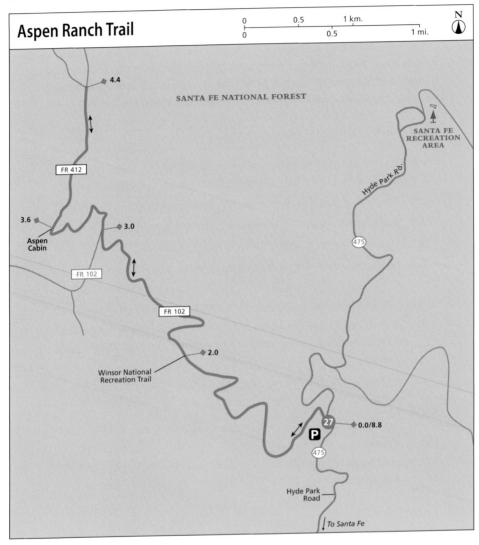

Aspen Ranch Trail

| 0 | | 0.5 | | 1 km. |
| 0 | | | 0.5 | 1 mi. |

N

4.4

SANTA FE NATIONAL FOREST

SANTA FE
RECREATION
AREA

Hyde Park Rd.

FR 412

475

3.6 ◆

3.0

Aspen
Cabin

FR 102

FR 102

2.0

Winsor National
Recreation Trail

27 ◆ 0.0/8.8

P

475

Hyde Park
Road

To Santa Fe

Restaurants

Cafe Pasqual's, 121 Don Gaspar Ave., Santa Fe; (505) 983-9340; www.pasquals
.com

The Cowgirl, 319 S Guadalupe St., Santa Fe; (505) 982-2465; www.cowgirl
santafe.com

La Casa Sena La Cantina, 125 E Palace Ave., Santa Fe; (505) 988-9232; www
.lacasasena.com

Big Tesuque Trail

The Big Tesuque Trail is rarely busy beyond its first 0.25 mile, and most of the traffic is on foot from the Big Tesuque Campground and Picnic Area. The trail whizzes down to Tesuque Creek and offers a tranquil spot to relax and cool off in the waters. This trail is for those who like to have their dessert first—the trail is all downhill for the first half and all uphill on a moderate climb all the way back to the Big Tesuque Trailhead.

Start: Big Tesuque Trailhead parking area, just off of Hyde Park Road (NM 475). The trail located across Hyde Park Road is labeled "Trail #152."

Length: 5.6 miles out and back

Riding time: 2 hours

Best bike: Mountain bike

Terrain and trail surface: A nice mix of rocky and smooth singletrack trails

Traffic and hazards: The trail is heavily used by other cyclists, trail runners, and day hikers.

Map: Dharma Maps, Santa Fe Explorer, 2012

Trail contacts: Santa Fe National Forest Headquarters, 11 Forest Ln., Santa Fe 87508; (505) 438-5300; www.fs.usda.gov/santafe

Special considerations: Restrooms, small tent campsites, and picnic tables are provided at the trailhead.

Getting there: From Santa Fe, take St. Francis Drive and turn right onto Paseo de Peralta. Drive 1.5 miles and turn right onto Bishop Lodge Road. Go 0.1 mile and turn right onto Artist Road, which becomes Hyde Park Road (NM 475). Continue straight for 11.7 miles to the Big Tesuque Trailhead and camping area, on the right. **GPS:** N35 46.156' / W105 48.553'

THE RIDE

The Tesuque Trail is very busy at the trailhead, mostly because it is easily accessed from the small campground and picnic area just across the street. Many school buses often line the parking area, and kids roast marshmallows in the heat of summer. But don't let this dissuade you; give the Big Tesuque Trail a chance.

Aspens flourish in this grassy meadow.

Beginning at the Big Tesuque parking and camping area, locate the Big Tesuque Trail (#152) across Hyde Park Road. A very steep rock staircase leads from the road down to the trail. Keep to the right of the North Branch of Tesuque Creek and continue on the Big Tesuque Trail. The trail gradually descends through a grassy area. At 0.3 mile the trail opens up to a small meadow as you pass through a national forest gate.

At 1.4 miles arrive at a three-way intersection. Turn left onto the Winsor National Recreation Trail (#254). Then at 1.6 miles stay left on the Winsor Trail as you pass an unmarked trail on the right. When the trail passes another small grassy meadow, you have gone 2.0 miles. At 2.4 miles the trail descends on super fun switchbacks; be careful—the trail may be a little loose and rocky. The trail reaches a three-way intersection at 2.7 miles. Turn left at the intersection onto Borrego Trail (#150). At just 2.8 miles the trail arrives at Tesuque Creek. The creek is canopied with old-growth trees and provides a perfect spot to take a dip in the warm summer months. Tesuque Creek also marks the spot of return; from here retrace the trail back to the parking area for a round-trip of 5.6 miles.

MILES AND DIRECTIONS

0.0 Start at the Big Tesuque Trailhead (Trail #152), across the street from the parking area on Hyde Park Road (NM 475), and begin downhill. You might need to carry your bike down the steep steps.

0.3 The trail crosses a national forest gate and continues straight into open meadow.

1.4 The trail intersects the Winsor National Recreation Trail; turn left onto Winsor.

1.6 Pass an unmarked trail on right; keep left on the Winsor Trail.

2.0 Enter a small grassy meadow.

2.4 Begin switchbacks.

2.7 Arrive at the intersection of the Winsor and Borrego Trails. Turn left onto Borrego.

Big Tesuque Trail

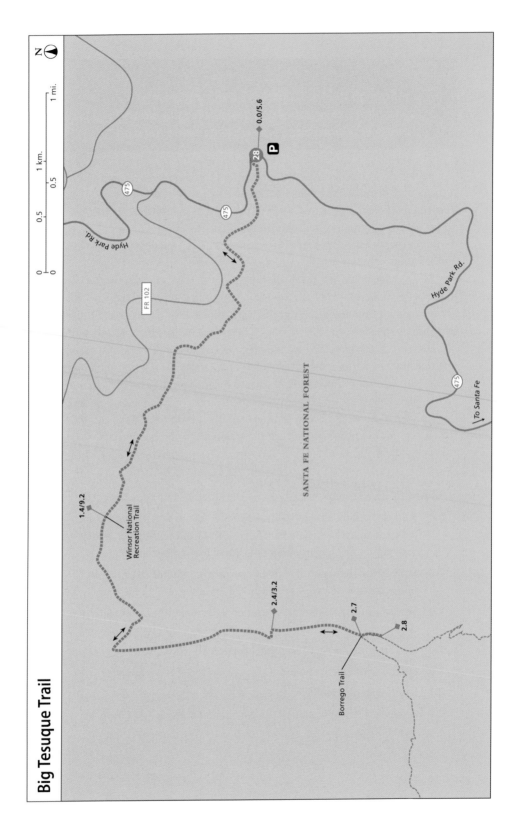

2.8 The Tesuque Creek welcomes you to the turnaround point. Turn around and retrace the trail back to the parking area.

5.6 Arrive back at the Big Tesuque parking area.

RIDE INFORMATION

Local Attraction
Turquoise Trail National Scenic Byway, NM 14 from Albuquerque to Santa Fe; Turquoise Trail Association; (505) 281-5233; www.turquoisetrail.org

Local Bike Shops
Mellow Velo Bicycles, 132 E Marcy St., Santa Fe; (505) 995-8356; www.mellowvelo.com
REI, 500 Markey St., Santa Fe; (505) 982-3557; www.rei.com
Sirius Cycles Bicycle Shop, 2801 Rodeo Rd., Santa Fe; (505) 819-7311; http://sirius-cycles.com
SpinDoc, 628 Old Las Vegas Hwy., Santa Fe; (505) 819-7311; www.spindoc.com

Restaurants
Bumble Bee's Baja Grill, 301 Jefferson St., Santa Fe; (505) 820-2862; www.bumblebeesbajagrill.com
Harry's Roadhouse, 96B Old Las Vegas Hwy., Santa Fe; (505) 989-4629; www.harrysroadhousesantafe.com
Jambo Cafe, 2010 Cerrillos Rd., Santa Fe; (505) 473-1269; www.jambocafe.net
The Shed, 113½ E Palace Ave., Santa Fe; (505) 982-9030; www.sfshed.com

Chamisa Trail

The Chamisa Trail (#183) goes through a ponderosa pine and mixed-conifer forest just east of Santa Fe. The short drive from downtown Santa Fe to the trailhead and the short length of the loop described here make this an ideal getaway when you need that quick fix but don't have a lot of time.

Start: Chamisa Trail Trailhead parking area, on the north side of Hyde Park Road

Length: 2.6-mile loop

Riding time: 1 hour

Best bike: Mountain bike

Terrain and trail surface: Packed-dirt singletrack the entire trail; narrow trail along mountainside on the first section and a few technical downhills on the return

Traffic and hazards: Motorized vehicles are not permitted on the trail. Riders may encounter hikers and equestrians.

Maps: USGS Santa Fe; Dharma Maps, Santa Fe Explorer, 2012

Trail contacts: Santa Fe National Forest Headquarters, 11 Forest Ln., Santa Fe 87508; (505) 438-5300; www.fs.usda.gov/santafe

Special considerations: Trail may be snowy and icy in winter.

Getting there: From Santa Fe, take St. Francis Drive and turn right onto Paseo de Peralta. Drive 1.5 miles and turn right onto Bishop Lodge Road. Go 0.1 mile and turn right onto Artist Road, which becomes Hyde Park Road (NM 475). Continue straight for 5.5 miles to the Chamisa Trailhead parking area, on the left. **GPS:** N35 43.725' / W105 51.968'

THE RIDE

Two trails leave from the Chamisa Trail parking area, located right off Hyde Park road. The main Chamisa Trail leaves the northeast corner of the parking area and goes uphill and east through the trees; the alternate route runs north through the canyon. The alternate route connects with the Chamisa Trail at a saddle about 1.0 mile from the trailhead. As described here, this alternate route can be used to make a fun training loop from the trailhead and back again. The first 0.25 mile of the Chamisa Trail climbs steadily from the parking area.

Chamisa Trail

Begin riding east on the clearly signed Chamisa Trail from the northeast corner of the parking area. The first 0.25 mile climbs steadily. The climb is somewhat steep, but this short stretch should not turn anyone back. The trail levels out and is almost flat for the next mile when you reach the top of the ridge and the saddle. At the saddle the trail makes a U-turn to the left (west and then south) onto the "alternate trail" at 1.5 miles. Left (west) is the Saddleback Trail; to the right (northeast) the Chamisa Trail continues north and drops down into a draw all the way to Tesuque Creek and the intersection with the Winsor National Recreation Trail (#254).

After making the U-turn onto the alternate trail, continue riding south as the trail begins dropping down into a canyon. There are a few technical parts through this section, so take it slow if you are not experienced. At 1.7 miles you reach the canyon floor and begin riding along the trail as it jumps in and out of the draw. The trail opens up into a meadow-like area at 2.4 miles and cruises to the trailhead parking area at 2.6 miles. Get ready for round two if time permits!

MILES AND DIRECTIONS

0.0 Start from the trailhead and begin riding right (east) on the Chamisa Trail.

1.5 Arrive at a trail junction. Make a sharp left to return to the trailhead and parking area via the alternate route. Left (west) is the Saddleback Trail; the Chamisa Trail continues right (northeast).

1.7 Reach the canyon floor.

2.6 Arrive back at the Chamisa Trailhead parking area.

RIDE INFORMATION

Local Attraction
Ski Santa Fe New Mexico, 1477 Hwy. 475, Santa Fe 87501; (505) 988-9636; http://skisantafe.com

Local Bike Shops
The Broken Spoke, 1426 Cerrillos Rd., Santa Fe; (505) 992-3102; http://broken spokesantafe.com
New Mexico Bike and Sport, 524 W Cordova Rd., Santa Fe; (505) 820-0809; http://nmbikensport.com
Rob and Charlie's, 1632 St. Michaels Drive, Santa Fe; (505) 471-9119; www.robandcharlies.com

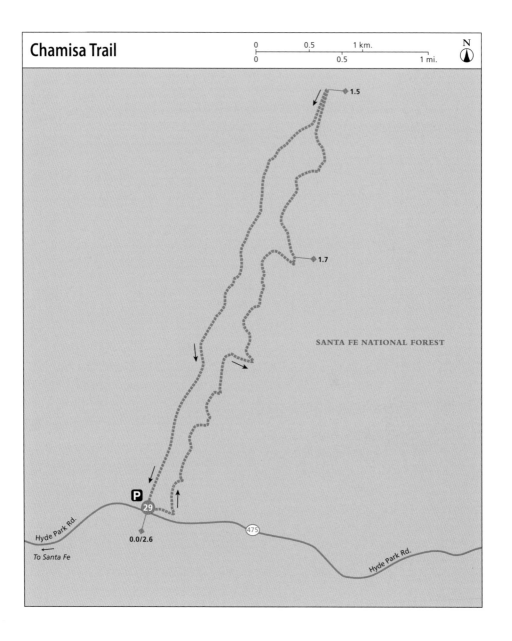

Chamisa Trail

SANTA FE NATIONAL FOREST

1.5

1.7

29 0.0/2.6

Hyde Park Rd.

To Santa Fe

475

Hyde Park Rd.

0   0.5   1 km.

0   0.5   1 mi.

N

Restaurants

Cafe Pasqual's, 121 Don Gaspar Ave., Santa Fe; (505) 983-9340; www.pasquals
.com

The Cowgirl, 319 S Guadalupe St., Santa Fe, NM; (505) 982-2465; www.cowgirl
santafe.com

La Casa Sena La Cantina, 125 E Palace Ave., Santa Fe; (505) 988-9232; www
.lacasasena.com

Hyde Park Road Summit

The Hyde Park Road Summit is great for cyclists looking to get their thighs burning and gain some major elevation. Hyde Park curves and climbs for almost 10 miles, beginning around 7,850 feet and climbing to over 10,350 feet. The great thing about Hyde Park is that after your climb, you get to reap the rewards as the road descends all the way back to the trailhead.

Start: Chamisa Trailhead, gravel parking area on Hyde Park Road (NM 475)

Length: 19.2 miles out and back

Riding time: 7 to 8 hours

Best bike: Road bike

Terrain and trail surface: Great big climbs on the paved Hyde Park Road (NM 475)

Traffic and hazards: The road is heavily used by motor vehicles and other cyclists.

Map: Dharma Maps, Santa Fe Explorer, 2012

Trail contacts: Santa Fe National Forest Headquarters, 11 Forest Ln., Santa Fe 87508; (505) 438-5300; www.fs.usda.gov/santafe

Special considerations: Bring food and extra water. Restrooms are frequent along the road. Late spring through fall are great times to ride Hyde Park.

Getting there: From Santa Fe, take St. Francis Drive and turn right onto Paseo de Peralta. Drive 1.5 miles and turn right onto Bishop Lodge Road. Go 0.1 mile and turn right onto Artist Road, which becomes Hyde Park Road (NM 475). Continue straight for 5.5 miles to the Chamisa Trailhead parking area, on the left. **GPS:** N35 43.725' / W105 51.968'

THE RIDE

The Hyde Park Road Summit is a local favorite, and cyclists can be seen climbing to the summit soon after spring has melted the snow away. Though the trail may be bustling with traffic in the peak season, the traffic tends to be slower for most of the route. There are also many places to stop and explore along the climb. Stop by the Hyde Memorial State Park Visitor Center on your

Hyde Park Road curves as it climbs to the summit.

> 🌿 **Riding Tip**
> *Riding conditioning: Riding is the best way to get in shape for riding, but a good strong core will take you a long way. Try lunges, sit-ups, and push-ups for starters. We recommend Tina Vindum's exercise guide, Outdoor Fitness, for a well-rounded approach to getting into shape for outdoor adventures.*

way up and talk to the friendly staff. Restrooms are also abundant along the route, so there is no worrying when you got to go.

Take a left out of the Chamisa Trail parking area onto Hyde Park Road (NM 475). The road begins at an elevation of about 7,850 feet. The road gradually climbs as it winds for the first 2.5 miles. At 1.6 miles the road enters Hyde Memorial State Park; the visitor center is on the right. Campgrounds run parallel to the road at 2.0 miles.

At mile 3.0 the road achieves a 14 percent gradient. The road keeps climbing as it reaches a nice viewpoint on the left at 4.0 miles—a nice spot to rest your legs. At 5.8 miles the road flattens out for a just a moment. Big Tesuque Campground and Picnic Area, on the right, mark the 6.3-mile mark. The campground offers restrooms, just off the road. The road passes the Aspen Vista Trailhead and Picnic Area, which offers a nice shaded area and restrooms, on the right at 7.5 miles.

The road finally offers some relief for your legs as the road reaches a nice big downhill section at 8.5 miles. After this, the road begins to climb once again. At 9.1 miles keep right at the split in the road. Pass the Santa Fe ski area on the right at 9.3 miles and continue on Hyde Park Road as it loops back around to the split. Keep right at the split and retrace the road as it begins its descent to the Chamisa Trailhead for a round-trip of 19.2 miles.

MILES AND DIRECTIONS

0.0 Start at the Chamisa Trailhead parking area and turn left onto Hyde Park Road (NM 475).

1.6 Enter Hyde Memorial State Park; the visitor center is on the right.

6.3 Pass Big Tesuque Campground and Picnic Area, on the right.

7.5 Arrive at the Aspen Vista Trailhead and Picnic Area, on the right.

9.1 When the road splits, keep right to the Santa Fe ski area.

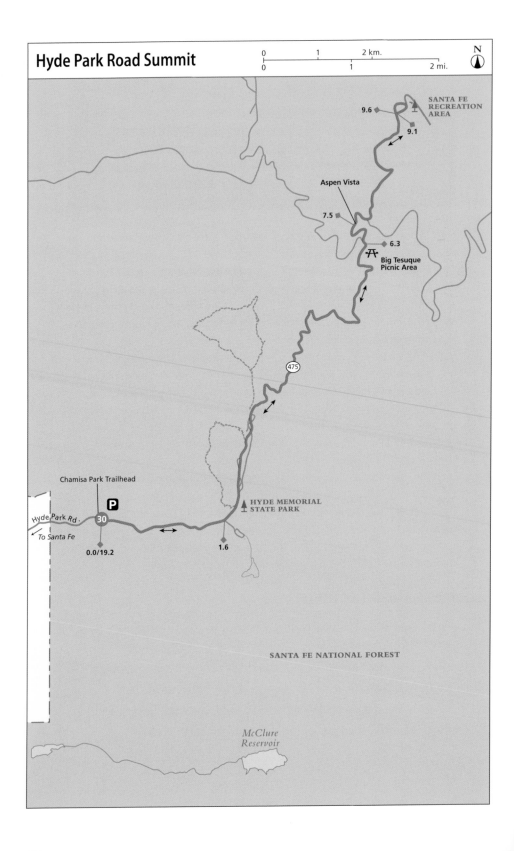

Hyde Park Road Summit

0   1   2 km.
0   1   2 mi.

N

SANTA FE
RECREATION
AREA

9.6

9.1

Aspen Vista

7.5

6.3

Big Tesuque
Picnic Area

475

Chamisa Park Trailhead

P

Hyde Park Rd.

30

To Santa Fe

0.0/19.2

HYDE MEMORIAL
STATE PARK

1.6

SANTA FE NATIONAL FOREST

McClure
Reservoir

9.6 After the road loops back around to the split, keep right on Hyde Park Road and begin the descent.

19.2 Arrive back at the Chamisa Trailhead parking area.

RIDE INFORMATION

Local Attraction

Wheelwright Museum of the American Indian, 704 Camino Lejo, Santa Fe; (505) 982-4636; https://wheelwright.org

Local Bike Shops

Mellow Velo Bicycles, 132 E Marcy Street, Santa Fe; (505) 995-8356; www.mellowvelo.com

REI, 500 Markey St., Santa Fe; (505) 982-3557; www.rei.com

Sirius Cycles Bicycle Shop, 2801 Rodeo Rd., Santa Fe; (505) 819-7311; http://sirius-cycles.com

SpinDoc, 628 Old Las Vegas Hwy., Santa Fe; (505) 819-7311; www.spindoc.com

Restaurants

Bumble Bee's Baja Grill, 301 Jefferson St., Santa Fe; (505) 820-2862; www.bumblebeesbajagrill.com

Harry's Roadhouse, 96B Old Las Vegas Hwy., Santa Fe; (505) 989-4629; www.harrysroadhousesantafe.com

Jambo Cafe, 2010 Cerrillos Rd., Santa Fe; (505) 473-1269; www.jambocafe.net

The Shed, 113½ E Palace Ave., Santa Fe; (505) 982-9030; www.sfshed.com

La Tierra Loop

The La Tierra Trails System spreads over 1,500 acres and contains over 25 miles of beautiful singletrack trails. This trail system is great for everyone, from beginner to advanced cyclist. The La Tierra Trails are one of the newest additions to the Santa Fe area trail system. Cyclists can enjoy riding through rolling hills and navigating arroyos, and some may even find solitude on a busy weekend afternoon with all the trail options La Tierra has to offer. Even if the trails are busy, they provide cyclists with an excellent escape and beautiful views.

Start: La Cuchara Trailhead, off NM 599

Length: 10.0-mile double loop

Riding time: 2 hours

Best bike: Mountain bike

Terrain and trail surface: Smooth and compacted sandy singletrack; some rocky areas

Traffic and hazards: Expect to encounter hikers and other cyclists. Horses, ATVs, and MX vehicles are allowed in designated park areas.

Maps: Free trail map available at the Santa Fe visitor center; map posted at each trail junction marker

Trail contacts: City of Santa Fe Parks Division, 200 Lincoln Ave., Santa Fe 87501; (505) 955-2100; www.santafenm.gov/trails

Special considerations: Bring extra water and sunscreen; shade is sparse on this trail system. Avoid areas under construction.

Getting there: From Santa Fe, take St. Francis Road to US 84 North; merge right onto NM 599 South. Continue for 2.5 miles and exit right onto Camino de los Montoyas. Turn left immediately onto La Cuchara Road. Follow La Cuchara Road for 0.2 mile and pass a school on the left. After the school you arrive at the nicely groomed La Cuchara Trailhead parking area. **GPS:** N35 42.556' / W105 58.015'

THE RIDE

The La Tierra Trails System is far different than the many other trails you will find in the Santa Fe area. Compared to the trails in the Santa Fe National Forest, the trails at La Tierra are smooth, hoppy, and very playful to ride on. Plus these trails are on nice sandy compact surfaces that provide great traction as you glide on the downhill sections and whip through the uphills.

The La Tierra trails are easily accessible, and it is very easy to find your way around. Trail junctions are numbered, and they seem to be at every corner. These trail junctions also contain very detailed maps of the area, so you always know where you are, even when you don't. Cyclists should be aware that there are several unregulated trails throughout the La Tierra system. However, all of these trails have been posted with signs to caution trail users.

The trails can get busy, but most riders would never know it with all the trail options La Tierra provides. These trails are also representative of what New Mexico mountain biking is all about. They offer endless views, arroyos, and some sand pit navigation, depending on the last rain. This type of riding is great because you can do it almost year-round and in open sunny skies.

This La Tierra loop encompasses all the outermost trails in the system. The trail begins to the left of the information board, at the small gate that leads down a gravel path. From the gate head straight on this path until you pass the trail junction (TJ) #24 post on your right; take the next singletrack on the right to TJ #21, at 400 feet.

The trail enters an open meadow and climbs gradually. At 0.2 mile a small trail appears on the left; keep straight. Arrive at TJ #21 at 0.6 mile and go left on the singletrack to TJ #19. at 0.9 mile arrive at TJ #19 and turn left to TJ #18.

Pass a trail at 1.4 miles and keep left to TJ #18. At 1.6 miles arrive at TJ #18 and proceed right.

At mile 1.7 you cross the first arroyo; keep straight. (**Note:** This area of the trail is scheduled for future improvements, so this might change.) Soon after this you see a trail on your right. Keep left to TJ #17; arrive at TJ #17 at 2.1 miles and make a left to TJ #16. At 2.3 miles arrive at TJ #16; continue straight to TJ #14.

> ### 🌿 Green Tip
> *Consider the packaging of any products you bring with you. Repack your provisions in zip-lock bags that you can reuse and that can double as garbage bags on the way out of the woods. If you took it on the trail, pack it out with you.*

Snow still lingers at the Santa Fe ski area in June.

Arrive at TJ #14 at 2.5 miles and keep left to TJ #13. This area of the La Tierra Trails is very nice, with an easy gradual ride. Piñon-junipers can be found all around you as you glide through this area. It won't be long before you arrive at TJ #13 at 3.0 miles. Keep left at this point until you reach TJ #5.

At 3.2 miles you reach TJ #5 and keep straight to TJ #3. At 3.5 miles go right to TJ #3. Arrive at TJ #3 at 3.6 miles and go right to TJ #2. At 4.3 miles you arrive at TJ #2; go left to TJ #1. The trail reaches TJ #1 at 5.3 miles. Go straight and cross Camino de los Montoyas and locate TJ #30 at the end of the Cala-basas parking area and trailhead. At TJ #30 turn right to TJ #31 and arrive at TJ #31 at 5.5 miles.

From TJ #31 go left to TJ #32. The TJ #32 trail is to the left of the cell tower and runs along the fence. Reach TJ #32 at 5.8 miles and continue straight to TJ #34, which you reach at 6.0 miles. From TJ #34 turn right toward TJ #36; arrive at TJ #36 at 6.6 miles then continue right to TJ #37. Reach TJ #37 at 6.9 miles; go right and continue straight as you pass TJ #35 at 7.2 miles. Continue straight past TJ #33 at 7.4 miles. Then at 7.7 miles arrive at a doubletrack dirt road; go left to find the trail to TJ #31. In 50 feet arrive at TJ #31 and go right to TJ #30. At 7.8 miles arrive at TJ #30; turn left and cross Camino de los Montoyas at the Calabasas Trailhead. The trail arrives back to TJ #1 at 7.9 miles. At the junction look behind you on the left and follow this trail to TJ #8. The trail reaches TJ #8 at 8.2 miles; turn left to TJ #9. At 8.5 miles keep straight to TJ #10 as the trail passes TJ #9.

At 8.7 miles arrive at TJ #10 and continue straight to TJ #11. The trail reaches TJ #11 at 8.9 miles. Go straight to TJ #21 and at 9.3 miles arrive at TJ #21. Take the far left route to TJ #23. Keep straight at 9.4 miles to TJs #24 and #23. At 9.8 miles stay left to TJ #24. Once the trail is no longer singletrack, make a left turn to the trailhead. Arrive back at the La Cuchara Trailhead at 10 miles.

MILES AND DIRECTIONS

0.0 Start to the left of the information board, at the small gate that leads down a gravel path. Head straight on this path until you pass the TJ #24 post, on your right. Take the next singletrack on the right to TJ #21 at 400 feet.

0.2 A small trail appears on the left; keep straight.

0.6 Arrive at TJ #21; go left on the singletrack to TJ #19.

0.9 Arrive at TJ #19; turn left to TJ #18.

1.4 Keep left to TJ #18.

1.6 Arrive at TJ #18 and proceed right.

1.7 Cross an arroyo and keep straight. Soon after this, a trail will be on your right; stay left to TJ #17.

2.1 Arrive at TJ #17. Make a left to TJ #16.

2.3 The trail reaches TJ #16 and continues straight to TJ #14.

2.5 Arrive at TJ #14 and keep left to TJ #13.

3.0 Arrive at TJ #13. Keep left until you reach TJ #5.

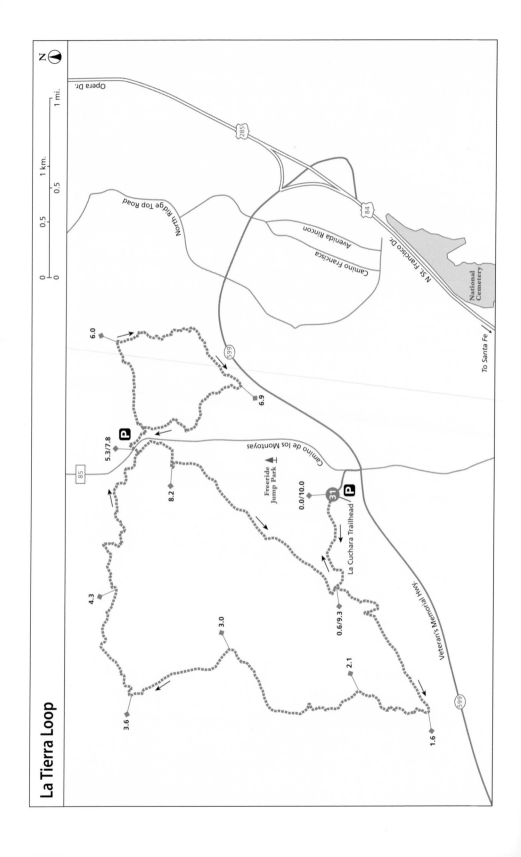

La Tierra Loop

3.2   Reach TJ #5 and keep straight to TJ #3.

3.5   Go right to TJ #3.

3.6   Arrive at TJ #3; go right to TJ #2.

4.3   Reach TJ #2; head left to TJ #1.

5.3   The trail arrives at TJ #1. Cross Camino de los Montoyas and locate TJ #30.

5.4   At TJ #30 turn right to TJ #31.

5.5   Arrive at TJ #31. Make a left to TJ #32, which runs to the left of the cell tower.

5.8   Reach TJ #32 at 5.8 miles and continue straight to TJ #34.

6.0   Arrive at TJ #34; turn right to TJ #36.

6.6   Arrive at TJ #36 and continue right to TJ #37.

6.9   Reach TJ #37; go right.

7.2   Continue straight as you pass TJ #35.

7.4   Continue straight as you pass TJs #33.

7.7   Arrive at a doubletrack dirt road; go left to find the trail to TJ #31. In 50 feet arrive at TJ #31; go right to TJ #30.

7.8   Arrive at TJ #30; turn left and cross Camino de los Montoyas.

7.9   Return to TJ #1. At the junction look behind you on the left and follow this trail to TJ #8.

8.2   Reach TJ #8 and turn left to TJ #9.

8.5   Keep straight to TJ #10 as the trail passes TJ #9.

8.7   Arrive at TJ #10 and continue straight to TJ #11.

8.9   Reach TJ #11; go straight to TJ #21.

9.3   Arrive at TJ #21. Take the far left route to TJ #23.

9.4   Keep straight to TJs #24 and #23.

9.8   Stay left to TJ #24. Once the trail is no longer singletrack, make a left turn to the trailhead.

10.0   Arrive back at the La Cuchara Trailhead.

RIDE INFORMATION

Local Attraction

San Miguel Mission, 401 Old Santa Fe Trail, Santa Fe; (505) 983-3974; http://santafe.org/Visiting_Santa_Fe/Entertainment/Historic_Sites

Local Bike Shops

The Broken Spoke, 1426 Cerrillos Rd., Santa Fe; (505) 992-3102; http://broken spokesantafe.com

New Mexico Bike and Sport, 524 W Cordova Rd., Santa Fe; (505) 820-0809; http://nmbikensport.com

Rob and Charlie's, 1632 St. Michaels Dr., Santa Fe, NM; (505) 471-9119; www .robandcharlies.com

Restaurants

Cafe Pasqual's, 121 Don Gaspar Ave., Santa Fe; (505) 983-9340; www.pasquals .com

The Cowgirl, 319 S Guadalupe St., Santa Fe; (505) 982-2465; www.cowgirl santafe.com

La Casa Sena La Cantina, 125 E Palace Ave., Santa Fe; (505) 988-9232; www .lacasasena.com

Dale Ball North Trails

One of the most popular trail systems in Santa Fe, the Dale Ball North Trails provide cyclists with great singletrack trails that any city would be proud to call their own. Trails are mostly smooth and hard packed. Dale Ball North Trails also tend to stay dry well into the winter months, when other trail systems can be wet. These trails are mere minutes from the Santa Fe Plaza and offer a quick escape.

Start: Dale Ball Trails North/Sierra Del Norte parking area

Length: 3.6-mile loop

Riding time: 1 hour

Best bike: Mountain bike

Terrain and trail surface: Smooth sandy singletrack with some slightly rocky areas

Traffic and hazards: The trails are heavily used by other cyclists, trail runners, and day hikers.

Maps: Dharma Maps, Santa Fe Explorer, 2012; free trail map available at the Santa Fe visitor center; maps posted at each trail junction marker

Trail contacts: City of Santa Fe Parks Division, 200 Lincoln Ave., Santa Fe 87501; (505) 955-2100; www.santafenm.gov/trails

Special considerations: Leashed dogs allowed on the trails, and there is a leash-free dog area across the street from the parking area. Please pick up after your dog; waste bags are available in the parking area.

Getting there: From Santa Fe take St. Francis Drive and turn right onto Paseo de Peralta. Drive 1.5 miles and turn right onto Bishop Lodge Road. Go 0.1 mile and turn right onto Artist Road, which becomes Hyde Park Road (NM 475). Continue straight for 2.5 miles and turn left onto Sierra Del Norte. The parking area is located just 500 feet on the right. **GPS:** N35 42.626' / W105 53.998'

THE RIDE

The Dale Ball North Trail System weaves through piñon and offers sweeping views of Santa Fe and the Sangre de Cristo Mountains. The entire Dale Ball Trail System encompasses over 30 miles of trails, so there are an almost overwhelming number of trail options. The north side of Dale Ball is pretty moderate. Cyclists looking for more climbs and a longer loop should check out the

A gradual climb on Dale Ball North

> ### 🐾 Hiking with Pets
> *We love hiking with our pets! It's great exercise, and dogs are arguably the best hiking partners. They never complain, and they are always ready to thoroughly explore a new trail. If you choose to ride with your pet, please be a responsible pet owner. Always clean up after your pet, and keeping him under control at all times. Pet waste is smelly, unsightly, and a health hazard for both humans and wildlife. Keeping your pet on a leash or under voice control is the best way to ensure that your pet is safe and not a nuisance to other riders, hikers, or wildlife. By doing these two simple things, you are doing your part to ensure that trails remain open to both you and your four-legged friends.*

Dale Ball Central Trail System, which can be accessed from the same parking lot as Dale Ball North.

Traffic can be pretty constant on the Dale Ball North Trails, even on weekdays. Take your time and watch for other cyclists, as well as those on foot. Keep in mind that plenty of dogs use these trails as well.

Beginning at the Dale Ball North/Sierra Del Norte parking area, locate the trail junction (TJ) #9 trail across the street. The trail is located to the left of the dog roaming area. From TJ #9 go straight; the trail curves to the left and begins a slight climb until you arrive at TJ #8 at 0.2 mile. From TJ #8 turn left and begin climbing a series of switchbacks that will get your blood flowing early on this loop. At 0.5 mile the trail arrives at an unmarked intersection, perhaps once the placement for TJ #7. Turn right at this intersection and reach TJ #7 on top of the hill at 0.6 mile. Take a look around at this point—it's the first part of the trail that offers views of Santa Fe.

Once at TJ #7 turn right; the trail begins to ride the ridgeline and then initiates a slight downhill to TJ #6. Arrive at TJ #6 at 0.8 mile and turn left. Glide down this fun downhill section until you arrive at TJ #5 at 1.0 mile. Go right at TJ #5; the trail hugs the side of the mountain as it continues to descend gradually. At 1.6 miles reach a gate at TJ #4. The trail crosses Sierra Del Norte, continues straight, then climbs for a bit to reach TJ #3 at 1.8 miles. From TJ #3 stay to the left; the trail weaves up and down until you reach a split at 2.6 miles. The trail on the left is the La Piedra Trail; continue right from the split.

The trail begins its final descent and arrives at TJ #2 at 3.3 miles. From TJ #2 turn left and enjoy the tight singletrack turns as the trail descends even more. At 3.6 miles exit right into the Dale Ball North/Sierra Del Norte parking area.

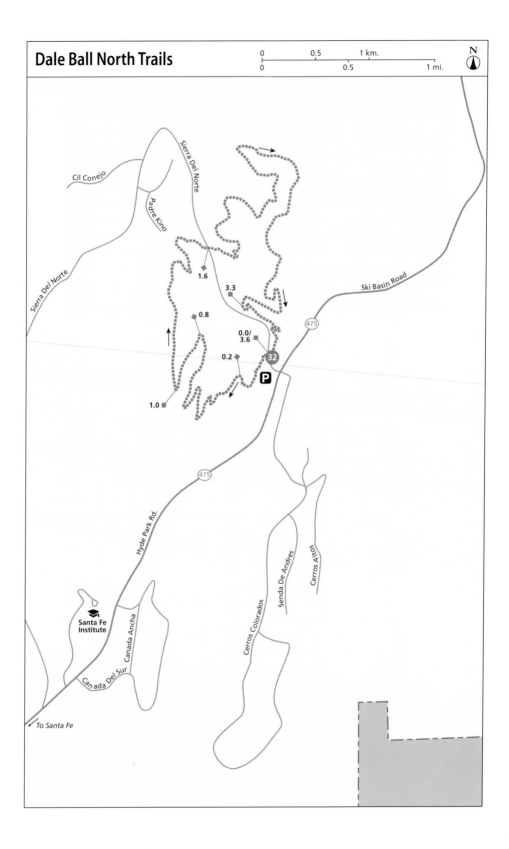

Dale Ball North Trails

MILES AND DIRECTIONS

0.0 Start at the Dale Ball Trails North/Sierra Del Norte parking area. Locate the TJ #9 trail across the street and go straight to TJ #8.

0.2 Arrive at TJ #8; go left.

0.5 At the intersection take the trail on the right uphill to TJ #7.

0.6 Arrive at TJ #7 and take the trail on the right.

0.8 Reach TJ #6 and take the trail on the left.

1.0 Arrives at TJ #5; go right.

1.3 Pass a wooden bench.

1.6 Reach TJ #4 at Sierra Del Norte. Cross the road and continue straight on the trail.

1.8 Arrive at TJ #3; stay left.

2.6 The trail splits at La Piedra Trail; stay right.

3.3 Reach TJ #2 and continue left.

3.6 Exit right to the Dale Ball Trails North/Sierra Del Norte parking area.

RIDE INFORMATION

Local Bike Shops

The Broken Spoke, 1426 Cerrillos Rd., Santa Fe; (505) 992-3102; http://broken spokesantafe.com

New Mexico Bike and Sport, 524 W Cordova Rd., Santa Fe; (505) 820-0809; http://nmbikensport.com

Rob and Charlie's, 1632 St. Michaels Dr., Santa Fe; (505) 471-9119; www.robandcharlies.com

Restaurants

Cafe Pasqual's, 121 Don Gaspar Ave., Santa Fe; (505) 983-9340; www.pasquals.com

The Cowgirl, 319 S Guadalupe St., Santa Fe; (505) 982-2465; www.cowgirl santafe.com

La Casa Sena La Cantina, 125 E Palace Ave., Santa Fe; (505) 988-9232; www.lacasasena.com

Dale Ball Central Trails

The Dale Ball Central Trails blend long moderate climbs with fun, zippy descents through piñon. The trails are very well marked, and there are trail maps at every junction, so it is very easy to find your way around. Not as busy as the north end, the Dale Ball Central Trails offer a little more solitude, if that is what you are seeking.

Start: Dale Ball Trails North/Sierra Del Norte parking area

Length: 6.2-mile loop

Riding time: 2 hours

Best bike: Mountain bike

Terrain and trail surface: Good climbs on this smooth sandy singletrack with some rocky areas

Traffic and hazards: These trails are heavily used by other cyclists, trail runners, and day hikers.

Maps: Dharma Maps, Santa Fe Explorer, 2012; free trail map available at the Santa Fe visitor center; maps posted at each trail junction marker

Trail contacts: City of Santa Fe Parks Division, 200 Lincoln Ave., Santa Fe 87501; (505) 955-2100; www.santafenm.gov/trails

Special considerations: Leashed dogs are allowed on the trails, and there is a leash-free dog roaming area located across the street from the parking area. Please pick up after your dog; waste bags are available in the parking area.

Getting there: From Santa Fe take St. Francis Drive and turn right onto Paseo de Peralta. Drive 1.5 miles and turn right onto Bishop Lodge Road. Go 0.1 mile and turn right onto Artist Road, which becomes Hyde Park Road (NM 475). Continue straight for 2.5 miles and turn left onto Sierra Del Norte. The parking area is located just 500 feet on the right. **GPS:** N35 42.625' / W105 53.979'

THE RIDE

The Dale Ball Central Trail System sees less traffic than Dale Ball North. The Central Trail System connects the North Dale to the South Dale Trail System; trail users can even ride to Atalaya Mountain from here with some pre-trip planning. Users also can cycle to the Randall David Audubon Center. Dale Ball Central is a super fun link that can be ridden in several different ways.

Smooth singletrack makes for a great climb.

The trail begins at the Dale Ball North/Sierra Del Norte parking area. Turn left onto Sierra Del Norte and head to the stop sign at Hyde Park Road (NM 475). At the stop sign continue straight across Hyde Park Road and locate trail junction (TJ) #13. From TJ #13 the trail dips into an arroyo. Once in the arroyo, the trail veers left and begins a gradual climb until TJ #12 at 0.6 mile. From TJ #12 the trail veers right and almost immediately arrives at TJ #11. The trail then turns left and begins a very short climb. After this short climb, follow the trail as it descends and reaches TJ #19 at 1.1 miles. From TJ #19 continue straight as the trail descends even more until you arrive at TJ #20 at 1.5 miles. Go right at TJ #20 and follow the arroyo until you reach TJ #24 at 1.7 miles. Continue straight, following the arroyo until you reach Cerro Gordo Road.

Reach Cerro Gordo Road at 2.2 miles and turn left. The road begins a small climb and then begins to descend. At 2.6 miles the road veers right on a sharp curve. Keep an eye out for the trail on the left at TJ #27; the trail junction is located next to a fence. As you pass through the fence, a steep climb awaits you. Once the trail begins to level out, the trail intersects TJ #26; go right. In 50 feet keep left as you pass The Nature Conservancy Trail on the right. The trail begins to weave in a series of switchbacks as you climb to 3.3 miles and arrive at TJ #25. Go right and prepare yourself for yet another climb on some smooth singletrack. At 3.7 reach TJ #23; continue straight as you pass an unmarked trail on the right. The trail eases out as you bike to TJ #22 at 3.9 miles; go right. Also keep right as you as you whiz pass TJ #16 at 4.1 miles. Before you know it the trail reaches TJ #15 at 4.2 miles; go right.

The trail climbs for 0.25 mile after TJ #15. After a sharp left turn, the trail descends to TJ #14 at 4.7 miles; go right. The trail begins a series of steep switchbacks and tight turns at 5.2 miles. After a fun descent, continue straight across Kachina Heights Drive at 5.7 miles. From this point on, the trail runs parallel to Hyde Park Drive and reaches TJ #13 again at 6.1 miles. Cross Hyde Park Road and follow your path back to the North Dale Ball/Sierra Del Norte parking area, where the journey ends at 6.2 miles.

MILES AND DIRECTIONS

0.0 Start from the Dale Ball North/Sierra Del Norte parking area. Turn left onto Sierra Del Norte and head to the stop sign at Hyde Park Road (NM 475).

0.1 At the stop sign continue straight across Hyde Park Road and locate TJ #13. Follow TJ #13 and stay left once in the arroyo.

0.6 At TJ #12 veer right.

0.7 At TJ #11 go left.

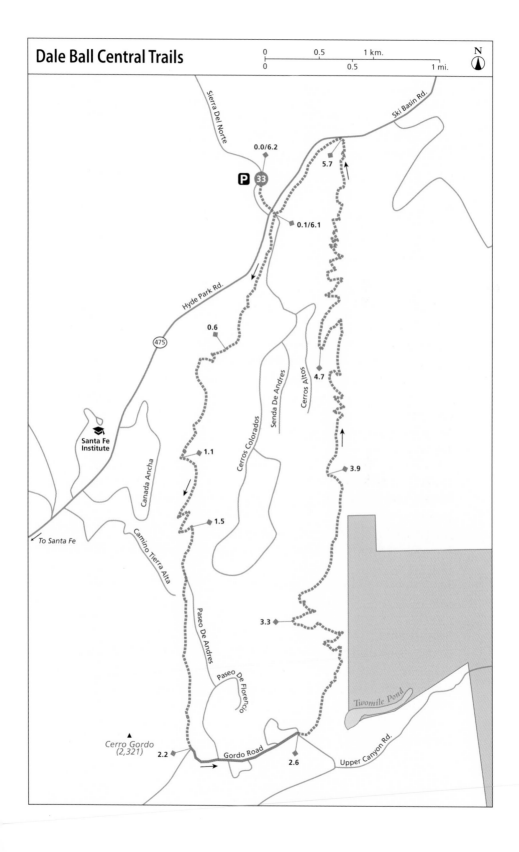

Dale Ball Central Trails

0   0.5   1 km.

0   0.5   1 mi.

N

Sierra Del Norte

Ski Basin Rd.

0.0/6.2

P 33

5.7

0.1/6.1

Hyde Park Rd.

475

0.6

4.7

Cerros Altos

Senda De Andres

Cerros Colorados

Santa Fe
Institute

1.1

3.9

Cañada Ancha

To Santa Fe

1.5

Camino Tierra Alta

3.3

Paseo De Andres

Paseo De Florencio

Twomile Pond

Cerro Gordo
(2,321)

2.2

Gordo Road

2.6

Upper Canyon Rd.

1.1 Arrive at TJ #19; continue straight.

1.5 Arrive at TJ #20; go right.

1.7 At TJ #24 go straight and follow the arroyo to Cerro Gordo Road.

2.2 Turn left onto Cerro Gordo Road.

2.6 Reach TJ #27 on the left after a sharp curve.

2.8 At TJ #26 go right and in 50 feet stay left as you pass The Nature Conservancy Trail.

3.3 At TJ #25 go right.

3.7 At TJ #23 continue straight, past an unmarked trail on the right.

3.9 At TJ #22 go right.

4.1 At TJ #16 go right.

4.2 At TJ #15 go right.

4.7 At TJ #14 go right.

5.7 Continue straight across Kachina Heights Drive. The trail runs parallel to Hyde Park Road until it reaches TJ #13.

6.1 Arrive at TJ #13; turn right and retrace the route back to parking area.

6.2 Arrive back at the Dale Ball North/Sierra Del Norte parking area.

RIDE INFORMATION

Local Bike Shops
Mellow Velo Bicycles, 132 E Marcy Street, Santa Fe; (505) 995-8356; www.mellowvelo.com
REI, 500 Markey St., Santa Fe; (505) 982-3557; www.rei.com
Sirius Cycles Bicycle Shop, 2801 Rodeo Rd., Santa Fe; (505) 819-7311; http://sirius-cycles.com
SpinDoc, 628 Old Las Vegas Hwy., Santa Fe; (505) 819-7311; www.spindoc.com

Restaurants
Bumble Bee's Baja Grill, 301 Jefferson St., Santa Fe; (505) 820-2862; www.bumblebeesbajagrill.com
Harry's Roadhouse, 96B Old Las Vegas Hwy., Santa Fe; (505) 989-4629; www.harrysroadhousesantafe.com
Jambo Cafe, 2010 Cerrillos Rd., Santa Fe; (505) 473-1269; www.jambocafe.net
The Shed, 113½ E Palace Ave., Santa Fe; (505) 982-9030; www.sfshed.com

Dale Ball South–Camino Loop

The Dale Ball South–Camino Loop is great for those days when you can't decide whether to mountain or road bike. This loop has both of these options in one. Start the ride out on a mountainous singletrack and glide down an arroyo onto an unpaved road. The unpaved road eventually becomes a paved road, and at the end you have the option to keep on the paved road or ride along a groomed gravel trail all the way back to the trailhead.

Start: Dale Ball South Trailhead parking area on Camino De Cruz Blanca

Length: 4.0-mile loop

Riding time: 1.5 hours

Best bike: Mountain bike or road bike

Terrain and trail surface: Singletrack smooth and rocky dirt trails; paved road; gravel road

Traffic and hazards: Watch for traffic on the paved and gravel roads. These trails are also used by hikers and trail runners.

Map: Dharma Maps, Santa Fe Explorer, 2012

Trail contacts: City of Santa Fe Parks Division, 200 Lincoln Ave., Santa Fe 87501; (505) 955-2100; www.santafenm.gov/trails

Special considerations: The paved road section provides a small bicycling lane.

Getting there: From Santa Fe, at the intersection of Cordova Road and St. Francis Drive, follow Cordova Road. At 1 mile continue straight across Old Pecos Trail. Continue on Cordova until you reach a stop sign at a three-way intersection. Turn left onto Camino Corrales. Go straight across Old Santa Fe Trail and veer left to Garcia Street. At the next three-way intersection, turn right onto Camino del Monte Sol and then take the second road on the left, Camino de Cruz Blanca. Continue on Camino de Cruz Blanca for 0.9 mile to the Dale Ball South Trailhead parking area, on the left just before the end of the paved road. **GPS:** N35 40.231' / W105 54.039'

THE RIDE

The Dale Ball South–Camino Loop provides a great opportunity to pack a picnic and enjoy it at the Watershed Museum and Park. This luxuriously well-maintained park closes at dusk. There have been many reports of vandalism at the trailhead, so try not to leave any valuables inside your car.

Locate the trailhead on the far left side of the Dale Ball South parking area and follow the singletrack as it descends, sandwiched between two large wooden fences. At 0.2 mile the trail crosses an arroyo. After a steady climb the trail arrives at trail junction (TJ) #39 at 0.5 mile; turn left to TJ #38. Weave along

Views of the Watershed Museum and Upper Canyon Road

the hillside on this moderate portion of the trail. Reach TJ #38 at 0.9 mile and make a left turn. At 1.3 miles keep an eye out for a trail that turns to the left, but continue straight. Ride over a small but steep hill and ride through the arroyo at the bottom.

The trail reaches Upper Canyon Road at 1.6 miles. Turn left and continue straight on this unpaved road. Upper Canyon Road turns into a paved road and reaches a stop sign at 2.4 miles. To the right is the Watershed Park; turn left onto Camino Cabra. Camino Cabra provides a bike lane for most of this section, but it eventually disappears. Camino Cabra may be busy with traffic in the early evening. At 3.1 miles turn left onto Camino De Cruz Blanca. Pass St. John's College on the right and continue right on Camino De Cruz Blanca at 3.4 miles. You can also get off the road at this point and travel on the Camino De Cruz Blanca Trail, which runs parallel to the road. The trail is nicely groomed gravel. The road eventually reaches the Dale Ball South parking area, on the left, completing the loop at 4.0 miles.

MILES AND DIRECTIONS

0.0 Start from the trailhead on the far left side of the Dale Ball South parking area and descend between two wooden fences that run parallel along the trail.

0.5 Arrive at TJ #39 and turn left to TJ #38.

0.9 Come to TJ #38; turn left.

1.3 A trail veers to the left. Continue straight to ride down a small hill and bike through an arroyo.

1.6 Arrive at Upper Canyon Road; turn left.

2.4 At the stop sign, turn left onto Camino Cabra. The Watershed Museum and Park is on the right.

3.1 Turn left onto Camino De Cruz Blanca.

3.4 Stay right on Camino De Cruz Blanca, or take the Camino De Cruz Blanca Trail, which parallels the road.

4.0 Arrive back at the Dale Ball South Trailhead parking area.

RIDE INFORMATION

Local Attractions/Events
Georgia O'Keeffe Museum, 217 Johnson St., Santa Fe; (505) 946-1000; www.okeeffemuseum.org

Dale Ball South–Camino Loop

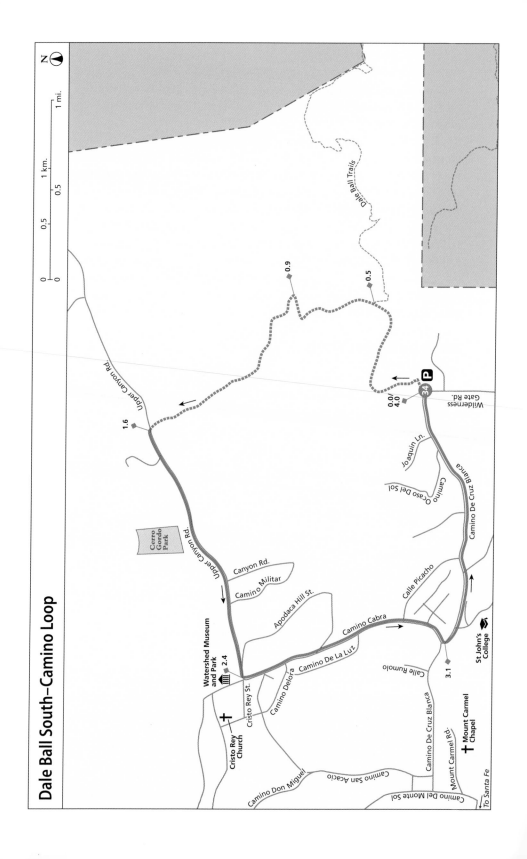

Museum of International Folk Art, 706 Camino Lejo, Santa Fe; (505) 476-1200; www.internationalfolkart.org

Local Bike Shops

The Broken Spoke, 1426 Cerrillos Rd., Santa Fe; (505) 992-3102; http://broken spokesantafe.com

New Mexico Bike and Sport, 524 W Cordova Rd., Santa Fe; (505) 820-0809; http://nmbikensport.com

Rob and Charlie's, 1632 St. Michaels Dr., Santa Fe; (505) 471-9119; www .robandcharlies.com

Restaurants

Cafe Pasqual's, 121 Don Gaspar Ave., Santa Fe; (505) 983-9340; www.pasquals .com

The Cowgirl, 319 S Guadalupe St., Santa Fe; (505) 982-2465; www.cowgirl santafe.com

La Casa Sena La Cantina, 125 E Palace Ave., Santa Fe; (505) 988-9232; www .lacasasena.com

Atalaya Mountain Trail

The Atalaya Mountain trail can be very technical and strenuous for most cyclists. Though the trail may seem easy in the beginning, switchbacks climb their way to the summit and seem to go on forever. The trail climbs more than 1,700 feet in just 3.8 miles, and most of the climbing is in the final push to the summit. The views from the summit are astounding and well worth the effort it takes to bike this local Santa Fe favorite. From the smooth singletracks of the arroyos to the rock-hopping trails nearing the summit, this trail has it all for riders looking for a great and rewarding challenge.

Start: St. Johns College/Atalaya Trailhead and visitor parking area on the St. John College campus

Length: 7.6-mile loop

Riding time: 2.5 to 3 hours

Best bike: Mountain bike

Terrain and trail surface: Smooth sandy singletrack in arroyos, some highly rocky areas along the trail to the summit

Traffic and hazards: The trail is heavily used by other cyclists, trail runners, and day hikers.

Map: Dharma Maps, Santa Fe Explorer, 2012

Trail contacts: Santa Fe National Forest, 1474 Rodeo Rd., Santa Fe 87501; (505) 438-7840; www.fs.fed.us/r3/sfe

Special considerations: No restrooms are available at the trailhead.

Getting there: From Santa Fe, at the intersection of Cordova Road and St. Francis Drive, follow Cordova Road. At 1 mile continue straight across Old Pecos Trail. Continue on Cordova until you reach a stop sign at a three-way intersection. Turn left onto Camino Corrales. Go straight across Old Santa Fe Trail and veer left to Garcia Street. At the next three-way intersection, turn right onto Camino del Monte Sol and then take the second road on the left, Camino de Cruz Blanca. In 0.2 mile turn right to St. John's College and then make an immediate right at the St. John's College welcome sign. The Atalaya Mountain Trailhead is located at the St. John's College campus visitor parking, on the left. **GPS:** N35 40.113' / W105 54.715'

THE RIDE

The Atalaya Mountain Trail has multiple trailheads. The St. John's College Trailhead is great because it offers abundant parking. The trail glides through a fun section of arroyos and gives cyclists the time to warm up before the climb begins to reach the summit at 9,121 feet. The Atalaya Trail can be very busy, even on weekdays. Try to ride in the morning or late afternoon to avoid the heavy foot traffic. Take your time on this trail, and bring extra snacks and plenty of water.

From the visitor parking area, locate the trailhead next to the information board; this is St. Johns Trail (#174). Proceed straight on the trail and veer right in 300 feet. The trail offers views of the St. Johns campus, and at 0.3 mile you near the edge of the campus and pass a bridge on your left. Keep straight at this point until 0.4 mile, where you veer left and cross an arroyo to continue on the trail.

The trail weaves you through arroyos shaded by piñon-junipers. This is especially nice on hot summer days when you're looking for relief from the sun. The trail begins to climb as you reach Wilderness Gate Road at 0.8 mile. Continue straight across this gravel-dirt road and carry your bike as you ascend the staircase. From the top of the staircase, the trail continues to the right.

Beginning around 1.0 mile, the trail becomes a series of switchbacks and you climb until you reach a large wooden fence on your right at 1.3 miles. Once through the fence, the trail starts to come to life, and bikers begin to realize the difficulty of the Atalaya Trail. At 1.5 miles continue straight as you

🐾 Green Tip
When you just have to go, dig a hole 6 to 8 inches deep and at least 200 feet from water, camps, and trails. Carry a zip-lock bag to carry out toilet paper, or use a natural substitute such as leaves instead (but not poison ivy!). Fill in the hole with soil and other natural materials when you're done.

A view from the Atalaya summit

pass an unmarked trail on the left. This unmarked trail leads to the Dorothy Stewart Trails System.

You have two options at 1.9 miles. The left fork is simply marked the "Harder Trail"; the right fork is labeled the "Easier Trail." The Harder Trail is shorter but much steeper and rockier than the Easier Trail. Although longer, the Easier Trail provides a more gradual incline so trail users can save their energy for the final push to the Atalaya summit. Both trails end at the same place, but take the Easier Trail on the right—it has better views.

At 2.5 miles the trail opens up for a moment, exiting the shadows of the ponderosa pines and Douglas firs onto a small bald. Take a break in this open area before the trail becomes a narrow singletrack. At 2.6 a steep route cuts back to the left. Continue straight at this point toward the summit. The trail begins a series of steep switchbacks at 3.0 miles. Rocks of all shapes and sizes abound, and the trail becomes even more difficult as you navigate your way around these obstacles. At 3.4 miles keep left to the summit, ignoring a small unmarked trail on the right that leads to a false summit.

Keep climbing. It won't get any easier until you reach the summit. The trail opens up to a small flat area at the summit. Boulder-size rocks lining the edges of the mountain are perfect for catching your breath and taking in the views. The trail continues from the summit and eventually connects to the Dale Ball South Trails System. Take your time as you retrace your route back to the parking

Best Bike Rides Albuquerque and Santa Fe

Atalaya Mountain Trail

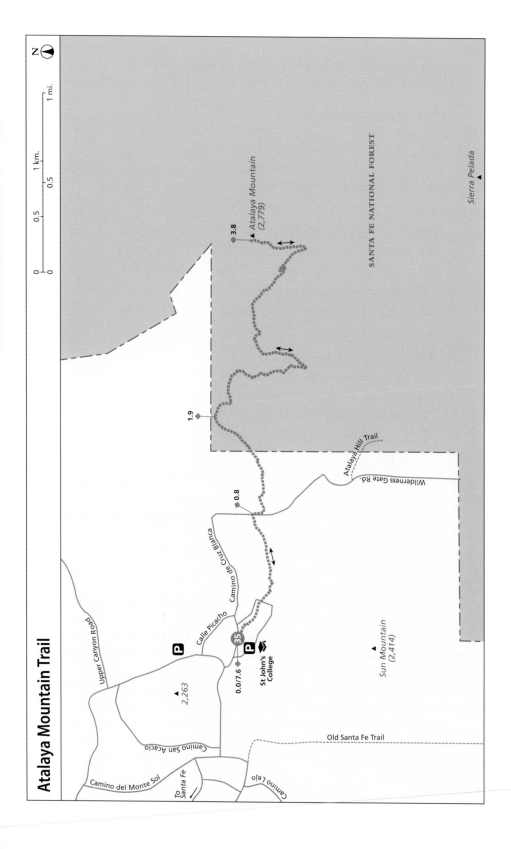

area—most of the trail is downhill. Please yield to other visitors as you navigate back down this steep, rocky descent to the trailhead for a round-trip of 7.6 miles.

MILES AND DIRECTIONS

- **0.0** Start from the St. John's College Trailhead and begin biking on Trail #174.
- **0.3** Pass a bridge on the left and continue straight.
- **0.4** Keep left across an arroyo to the trail.
- **0.8** Cross Wilderness Gate Road. Ascend the staircase and turn right.
- **1.3** Pass through a large wooden gate. Continue the ascent.
- **1.5** Continue straight as you pass a trail on the left.
- **1.9** The trail splits. Take the trail on the right, marked "Easier."
- **2.5** Reach an open bald. The trail continues on the right.
- **2.6** A steep trail appears on the left. Continue straight.
- **3.0** Begin steep switchbacks.
- **3.4** Ignore the unmarked trail on the right and keep left to the summit.
- **3.8** Reach the Atalaya Mountain summit. Rest and enjoy the views before carefully retracing your route back to the trailhead.
- **7.6** Arrive back at the trailhead parking area.

RIDE INFORMATION

Local Bike Shops
Mellow Velo Bicycles, 132 E Marcy St., Santa Fe; (505) 995-8356; www.mellow velo.com
REI, 500 Markey St., Santa Fe; (505) 982-3557; www.rei.com
Sirius Cycles Bicycle Shop, 2801 Rodeo Rd., Santa Fe; (505) 819-7311; http:// sirius-cycles.com
SpinDoc, 628 Old Las Vegas Hwy., Santa Fe; (505) 819-7311; www.spindoc.com

Restaurants
Bumble Bee's Baja Grill, 301 Jefferson St., Santa Fe; (505) 820-2862; www .bumblebeesbajagrill.com
Harry's Roadhouse, 96B Old Las Vegas Hwy., Santa Fe; (505) 989-4629; www .harrysroadhousesantafe.com
Jambo Cafe, 2010 Cerrillos Rd., Santa Fe; (505) 473-1269; www.jambocafe.net
The Shed, 113½ E Palace Ave., Santa Fe; (505) 982-9030; www.sfshed.com

Arroyo de los Chamisos Trail

The Arroyo de los Chamisos Trail is a great multiuse trail that runs through Santa Fe. Riders can access the trail from numerous locations and can enjoy attractions like Campanas Park.

Start: Parking area and trailhead at the northwest corner of South St. Francis Drive and West Zia Road

Length: 7.4 miles out and back

Riding time: 1.5 to 2 hours

Best bike: Hybrid

Terrain and trail surface: Paved trail that is mostly flat; a few road crossings

Traffic and hazards: Motorized vehicles are not permitted on the trail except for maintenance and emergency vehicles.

Maps: USGS Santa Fe; trail map available on City of Santa Fe website

Trail contacts: City of Santa Fe, 200 Lincoln Ave., Santa Fe 87501; (505) 955-6949; www.santafenm.gov/trails_1

Special considerations: The best time to ride without traffic is early in the morning.

Getting there: From downtown Santa Fe, drive south on South St. Francis Drive for about 2 miles to West Zia Road. Turn right (west) onto West Zia Road and then make an immediate right (north) into the unsigned parking area. **GPS:** N35 38.838' / W105 57.426'

THE RIDE

This multiuse recreation path follows along the Arroyo de los Chamisos, a major drainage system in the southeast part of Santa Fe. The Arroyo de los Chamisos Trail is a fun little ride on a well-maintained, smooth paved surface that follows the arroyo for 3.7 miles. This is a great ride for novice cyclists and for anyone who wants to get in a quick ride during the winter months, when most area bike trails are snowed in. The trail is also quite popular with walkers and runners and sees a lot of foot traffic during weekends and evenings.

From the parking area and trailhead at the northwest corner of South St. Francis Drive and West Zia Road in Santa Fe, begin riding north on the paved trail. The trail continues north for a short distance before turning west and then southwest. At 0.7 mile stay left (southwest) to ride through a tunnel. Right (north) is a parking area and trail access point. Continue riding and go under a second tunnel at 0.8 mile. This section of trail is pretty quiet, as the

Arroyo de los Chamisos Trail

neighborhoods are sparse until 1.2 miles, where you cross Yucca Street and get into some more heavily used sections of the trail.

Continue along the arroyo and cross Camino Carlos Rey at 1.8 miles and then Campanas Road at 2.2 miles. Immediately after crossing the road, you pass Campanas Park on the right (north). Plenty of rest stops, play areas, and even disc golf are available here. Keep west on the trail past the park, riding through another quiet section just before arriving at a busy business district. Ride under Rodeo Road at 3.5 miles as the trail turns south and arrives at Villa Linda Park at 3.7 miles. Turn around here and retrace your route to the trailhead parking area for a round-trip of 7.4 miles.

MILES AND DIRECTIONS

0.0 Start from the trailhead parking area and begin riding north on the paved trail.

0.7 Stay left (southwest) and ride through the tunnel. Right (north) leads to a parking area.

0.8 Ride through a second tunnel.

1.2 Cross over Yucca Street.

1.8 Cross over Camino Carlos Rey.

2.2 Cross Campanas Road and then ride past Campanas Park on the right (north).

3.5 Ride under Rodeo Road.

3.7 Arrive at Villa Linda Park. Turn around here and return via the same route.

7.4 Arrive back at the trailhead parking area.

RIDE INFORMATION

Local Attraction
Lensic Performing Arts Center, 211 W San Francisco St., Santa Fe 87501; (505) 988-7050; www.lensic.org

Local Bike Shops
The Broken Spoke, 1426 Cerrillos Rd., Santa Fe; (505) 992-3102; http://broken spokesantafe.com
New Mexico Bike and Sport, 524 W Cordova Rd., Santa Fe; (505) 820-0809; http://nmbikensport.com

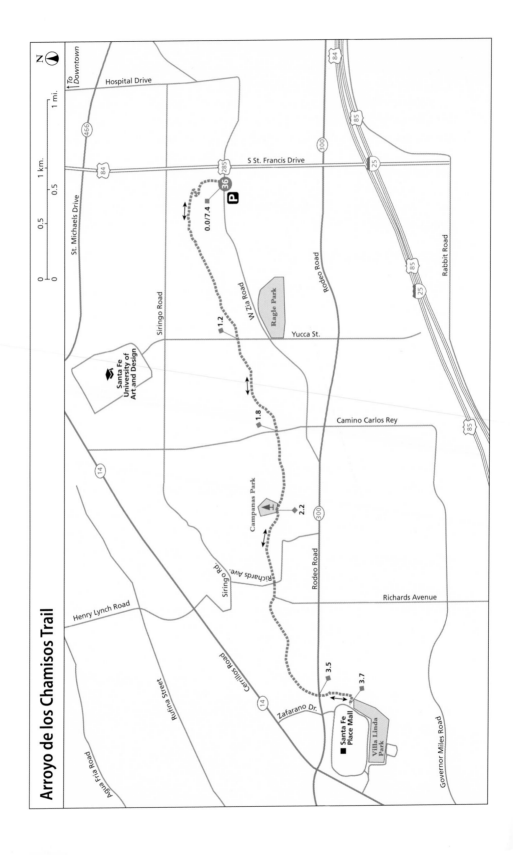

Arroyo de los Chamisos Trail

Rob and Charlie's, 1632 St. Michaels Dr., Santa Fe; (505) 471-9119; www.rob andcharlies.com

Restaurants

Cafe Pasqual's, 121 Don Gaspar Ave., Santa Fe; (505) 983-9340; www.pasquals .com

The Cowgirl, 319 S Guadalupe St., Santa Fe; (505) 982-2465; www.cowgirl santafe.com

La Casa Sena La Cantina, 125 E Palace Ave., Santa Fe; (505) 988-9232; www .lacasasena.com

Santa Fe Rail Trail

The wonderful Santa Fe Rail Trail travels along the historic Atchison, Topeka and Santa Fe Railway. The portion of the rail trail that is managed by the county and described here begins just south of the city and quickly takes riders into the beautiful rolling hills of the desert.

Start: Trailhead parking area, just south of Rabbit Road

Length: 23.6 miles out and back

Riding time: 4 to 6 hours

Best bike: Mountain bike

Terrain and trail surface: Gently rolling packed-dirt singletrack

Traffic and hazards: Motorized vehicles may be encountered on portions of the trail. Riders should expect to encounter hikers, runners, and equestrians.

Maps: USGS Santa Fe; map available for download at website

Trail contacts: Santa Fe County, 102 Grant Ave., Santa Fe 87501-2061; (505) 986-6200; www.santafecountynm.gov/public_works/open_space_and_trails_program

Special considerations: If you are planning a shuttle, cell phone reception may be an issue at the southern end of the described section.

Getting there: From Santa Fe, drive south on South St. Francis Drive for 3.5 miles. Turn right (west) onto Rabbit Road and continue west for 0.6 mile to the trailhead parking area, on the left (south). **GPS:** N35 37.867' / W105 57.909'

THE RIDE

The 17-mile-long Santa Fe Rail Trail follows the old Atchison, Topeka and Santa Fe Railway. The trail actually begins in Santa Fe Railyard Park and then continues along the tracks to US 285 through the small communities of El Dorado and Lamy. The trail features urban, suburban, and rural characteristics as it leaves Santa Fe and runs along hilly, red-dirt terrain through a countryside of yucca and green junipers.

The Santa Fe Rail Trail is paved and accessible between Railyard Park and the Rabbit Road access point. Beyond Rabbit Road the trail is unimproved and requires a mountain bike for ideal riding. South of Rabbit Road there are a few steep climbs, a couple of arroyo crossings, and plenty of goat heads to dodge. "Goat head" is the name that has been given to the large thorny seeds that can find their way into—and flatten—your bike tires. Trail managers have plans to resurface some areas of the Santa Fe Rail Trail to reduce erosion and make the trail safer.

From the trailhead parking area at Rabbit Road, begin riding south on the gravel trail. Views of the Cerrillos Hills and Sandia Mountains to the southwest are immediate and last throughout much of the ride, making the scenery a selling point. The trail starts with a fun descent to get you in the mood and then you reach the first of two railroad track crossings at 1.0 mile. Cross right (west) over the tracks and then turn left (south) to continue along them. The trail rolls through the countryside to 1.7 miles, where you should stay left (southwest) on the main trail. Right (west) leads to the Santa Fe Community College and a parking area and trailhead access point. The trail becomes a much more rugged singletrack trail.

The trail continues south through the juniper landscape and crosses Nine Mile Road at 2.8 miles. There is another parking area and trailhead here. After a long stretch of fun ups and downs and arroyo crossings, you cross over a

JD's Famous Trail Mix Recipe

One of our favorite mixes that we make at home comes from products we buy at the local natural foods store:

    2 cups salted cashews (JD likes honey roasted)
    1 cup raw macadamia nuts
    1 cup dried pineapple
    1 cup dried cranberries (JD likes orange flavored)
    1 cup dried mango
    1 cup Nature's Path granola (optional)

Beginner-friendly mountain biking on the Santa Fe Rail Trail

dirt road at 5.2 miles and then reach the second railroad track crossing at 6.2 miles. Cross left (east) over the tracks and then right (south) to continue along the trail. This area can look a little tricky, as a few other trails lead to and from the main trail. Just remember that your trail runs along the railroad tracks.

At 6.9 miles you come to a somewhat busy road crossing. Cross Vista Grande Avenue and stay to the left (east) of the tracks to continue on the rail trail. Come to a second road crossing at 8.6 miles and cross Eldorado Avenue, staying to the left (east) again. You encounter a few ups and downs through this stretch as well as a gravel road crossing at 10.1 miles. The trail then follows the tracks as it makes its final climb and then squeezes through a canyon before descending to US 285 at 11.8 miles. There is not much here at the end except the highway, so turn around and return to the trailhead parking area for a round-trip of 23.6 miles.

MILES AND DIRECTIONS

0.0 Start from the trailhead parking area at Rabbit Road and begin riding south on the gravel trail.

1.0 Cross right (west) over the railroad tracks.

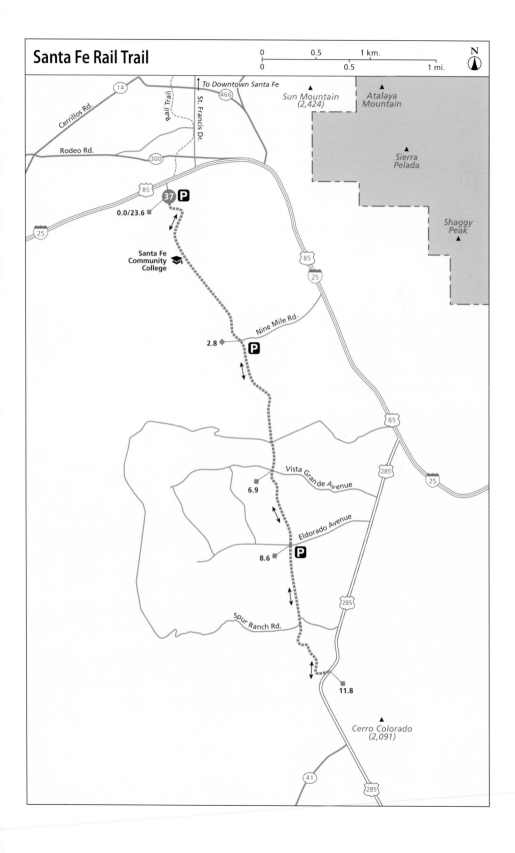

1.7 Stay left (southeast) on the main trail. Right (west) leads to the Santa Fe Community College Trailhead parking area.

2.8 Cross over Nine Mile Road and a trail access point on the left (east).

5.2 Cross a private drive and continue riding south.

6.2 Cross left (east) over the tracks and then turn right (south) to continue along the tracks.

6.9 Cross Vista Grande Avenue and stay on the left (east) side of the tracks.

8.6 Cross Eldorado Avenue, staying to the left (east) of the tracks again.

10.1 Cross a gravel road.

11.8 Reach US 285. Turn around here and return via the same route.

23.6 Arrive back at the trailhead parking area.

RIDE INFORMATION

Local Bike Shops
Mellow Velo Bicycles, 132 E Marcy St., Santa Fe; (505) 995-8356; www.mellowvelo.com
REI, 500 Markey St., Santa Fe; (505) 982-3557; www.rei.com
Sirius Cycles Bicycle Shop, 2801 Rodeo Rd., Santa Fe; (505) 819-7311; http://sirius-cycles.com
SpinDoc, 628 Old Las Vegas Hwy., Santa Fe; (505) 819-7311; www.spindoc.com

Restaurants
Bumble Bee's Baja Grill, 301 Jefferson St., Santa Fe; (505) 820-2862; www.bumblebeesbajagrill.com
Harry's Roadhouse, 96B Old Las Vegas Hwy., Santa Fe; (505) 989-4629; www.harrysroadhousesantafe.com
Jambo Cafe, 2010 Cerrillos Rd., Santa Fe; (505) 473-1269; www.jambocafe.net
The Shed, 113½ E Palace Ave, Santa Fe; (505) 982-9030; www.sfshed.com

Old Santa Fe and Pecos Trails

The Old Santa Fe and Pecos Trails offer a unique opportunity to retrace history, explore boutiques, and visit museums along the route. Take your time and explore the culture of the Southwest in the heart of Santa Fe. The ride traverses a moderate stretch of roadway outside Santa Fe Plaza, with some busy intersections along its route.

Start: Santa Fe Plaza, at the intersection of East San Francisco Street and the Old Santa Fe Trail

Length: 9.0 miles out and back.

Riding time: 1.5 to 2 hours

Best bike: Road bike

Terrain and trail surface: Gently rolling paved roads

Traffic and hazards: The trails are heavily used by motor vehicles and other cyclists.

Map: USGS Santa Fe

Trail contacts: New Mexico Department of Transportation, 1120 Cerrillos Rd., Santa Fe 87504; (505) 827-5100; dot.state.nm.us

Special considerations: The best time to ride without traffic is early morning.

Getting there: The ride begins at the Santa Fe Plaza. **GPS:** N35 41.233' / W105 56.350'

THE RIDE

The route starts at Santa Fe Plaza, one of the most historic and beautiful areas in all of New Mexico. From the local music to the Cathedral Basilica of St. Francis, everyone will find something worth exploring on this ride. Bring a camera and enjoy the vibrant colors and Spanish architecture that adorn the plaza. Although this route offers some beautiful sights, it also crosses a few busy intersections. Take your time and enjoy the ride.

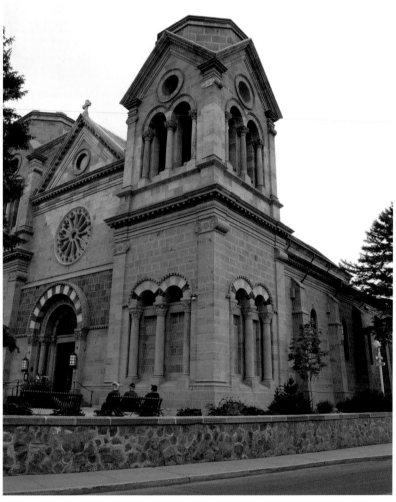

The Cathedral Basilica of St. Francis of Assisi is one of many sights along the Old Santa Fe Trail.

When you return to the Santa Fe Plaza, explore the many locally owned shops. Get a bite to eat—you deserve it after this long ride. Meet up with some friends and have a picnic in the plaza. There are so many options.

Beginning from the historic Santa Fe Plaza, locate the intersection of East San Francisco Street and Old Santa Fe Trail. Cross the Old Santa Fe Trail and continue straight to Cathedral Place toward the Cathedral Basilica of St. Francis of Assisi. At 0.1 mile turn right onto Cathedral Place and then make an immediate right onto East Water Street. At 0.2 mile make a left onto Old Santa Fe Trail and continue straight. Pass the Loretto Chapel on the left; on certain days artists set up and sell their artwork here. At 0.5 mile continue straight across the intersection at Paseo De Peralta.

Old Santa Fe veers off to the right at 1.0 mile; continue straight onto Old Pecos Trail. The road passes through many small intersections; remain straight the whole way. At 1.8 miles Old Pecos Trail crosses East San Mateo Road and continues straight. Keep straight again as Old Pecos Trail intersects Arroyo Chamiso Road. Old Pecos Trail veers left at 2.5 miles. Stay on Old Pecos Trail until it dead-ends at CR 58D, a dirt road. Turn around and retrace the route back to Santa Fe Plaza for a round-trip of 9.0 miles.

MILES AND DIRECTIONS

0.0 Start from Santa Fe Plaza and locate the intersection of East San Francisco Street and Old Santa Fe Trail. Cross Old Santa Fe Trail and continue straight to Cathedral Place.

0.1 Turn right onto Cathedral Place, and then make an immediate right onto East Water Street.

0.2 Make a left onto Old Santa Fe Trail and continue straight.

0.5 Continue straight across Paseo De Peralta.

1.0 Old Santa Fe Trail veers left; keep straight onto Old Pecos Trail.

1.8 Continue on Old Pecos Trail as the road crosses East San Mateo Road.

2.3 Keep straight on Old Pecos Trail as the road intersects Arroyo Chamiso Road.

2.5 Old Pecos Trail veers left.

4.5 Old Pecos Trail dead-ends at CR 58D. Turn around and retrace the route back to Santa Fe Plaza.

9.0 Arrive back at Santa Fe Plaza.

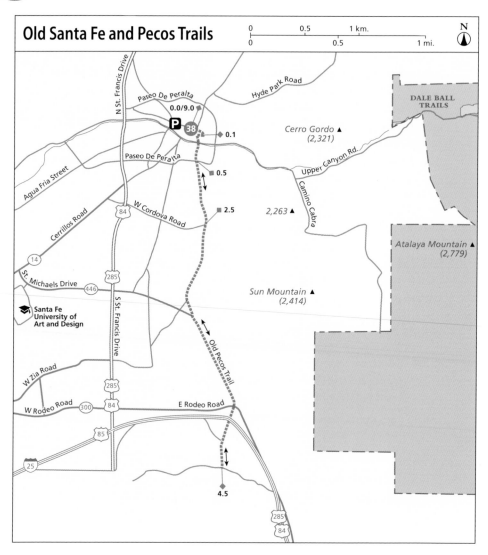

Old Santa Fe and Pecos Trails

RIDE INFORMATION

Local Bike Shops
The Broken Spoke, 1426 Cerrillos Rd., Santa Fe; (505) 992-3102; http://broken
spokesantafe.com
New Mexico Bike and Sport, 524 W Cordova Rd., Santa Fe; (505) 820-0809;
http://nmbikensport.com

Rob and Charlie's, 1632 St. Michaels Dr., Santa Fe; (505) 471-9119; www .robandcharlies.com

Restaurants

Cafe Pasqual's, 121 Don Gaspar Ave., Santa Fe; (505) 983-9340; www.pasquals .com

The Cowgirl, 319 S Guadalupe St., Santa Fe; (505) 982-2465; www.cowgirl santafe.com

La Casa Sena La Cantina, 125 E Palace Ave., Santa Fe; (505) 988-9232; www .lacasasena.com

Galisteo Basin Preserve Trails

The master plan for the Galisteo Basin Preserve Stewardship Community includes 50 miles of hiking, biking, and equestrian trails. Currently about 18 miles are open to the public, including this fun little 6.0-mile loop that connects a series of trails through the preserve.

Start: Northwest corner of the Thumb Trailhead parking area, on the west side of New Moon Overlook

Length: 6.0-mile loop

Riding time: 1 to 2 hours

Best bike: Mountain bike

Terrain and trail surface: Packed-dirt singletrack travels through canyons and along ridges

Traffic and hazards: No motorized vehicles are permitted on the trails. Riders may encounter hikers and equestrians.

Maps: USGS Santa Fe; trail map available for download on website

Trail contacts: Galisteo Basin Preserve, 117 N Guadalupe St., Ste. C, Santa Fe 87501; (505) 982-0071; www.galisteobasinpreserve.com/index .php

Special considerations: Not all trails are open to the public. Please respect Private Property signs and restrictions.

Getting there: From Santa Fe, drive south for 17.8 miles on US 84 and US 285 to Astral Valley Road and the signed access for Galisteo Basin Preserve. Turn right (west) onto Astral Valley Road and drive 0.2 mile to New Moon Overlook. Turn right (north) onto New Moon Overlook and drive 0.1 mile to the Thumb Trailhead parking area, on the left (west). **GPS:** N35 28.755' / W105 54.769'

THE RIDE

According to the official website, "the Galisteo Basin Preserve is the flagship initiative of Commonweal Conservancy, a nonprofit conservation-based community development organization." The Commonweal acquired the land that eventually became the Galisteo Basin Preserve in 2003. Since then, the conservation neighborhoods of West Basin, New Moon Overlook, Southern Crescent, East Preserve, and Conservation Ranches have all developed along with a small network of private and public access trails. The website hails the preserve as a "model for stewardship-based community development in the Southwest."

Begin riding north from the northwest corner of the Thumb Trailhead parking area, located west of the New Moon Overlook road. Turn right (northwest) onto Cooka's Loop East at 0.1 mile. Left (west) is Cooka's Loop West, your return trail. The trail heads uphill along a ridge and arrives at the first of many trail junctions at 0.5 mile. Stay right (north) on Cooka's Loop East. Left (west) shortcuts over to Cooka's Loop West. Continue north and then northwest along the trail to 0.7 mile. Stay left (west) here on Cooka's Loop. Right (north) is a private trail. From here the trail turns west and then southeast and goes down into the canyon you were just riding above. As the trail turns south and then southwest, turn right (west) onto Eliza's Ridge Trail at 1.0 mile. To the left (south), Cooka's Loop West heads back to the parking area and trailhead.

Eliza's Ridge Trail traverses a long ridge. At about 1.3 miles you come to a somewhat technical downhill where the trail then crosses a wash at the bottom. Cross the wash and stay to the right (north) on Eliza's Ridge Trail. Left (south) is the Sphinx Loop West. The trail follows along the canyon floor for a short distance and then climbs back up to the ridge at 1.9 miles, where you stay straight (northwest) on Eliza's Ridge Trail. Left (south) is Cosmo's Spur; right (north) is a private trail.

After a long stretch along the ridge, where the trail hugs several drop-offs, the trail turns south and you arrive at a trail junction. Stay left (south) at this junction on Eliza's Ridge Trail. Right (north) is Sophie's Spur trail. Descend the ridge to a low saddle and then turn left (southeast) onto the Shepherd's Trail. To the right (southwest) the Eliza's Ridge Trail continues to several other trails. The Shepherd's Trail continues downhill to the valley floor, weaves through numerous juniper trees, and crosses a few washes before reaching the North Wagon Trail at 3.8 miles. Turn left (north) onto the North Wagon Trail. Right (south) leads to the Cowboy Shack Trailhead parking area.

The doubletrack North Wagon Trail heads northeast across the valley floor. You hit a couple of trail junctions along this section. The first is at 4.4 miles, where you stay right (northeast) on the North Wagon Trail. Left (north)

View of the Cerrillos Hills and the Sandia Mountains

is the Cosmo's Spur trail. Reach another junction at 4.7 miles; stay left (north-east) on the North Wagon Trail. Right (south) leads to the Trenza Overlook and a trail access point. Shortly after, at 4.8 miles, turn right (east) onto the Sphinx Loop East. Left (northwest) is the Sphinx Loop West. The trail climbs steeply here and becomes quite narrow in a few spots, making it a pretty tough climb. At the top of climb you turn right (south) onto Cooka's Loop West and begin riding south as the trail levels out a bit. Left (north), Cooka's Loop West leads back to Eliza's Ridge Trail.

At 5.7 miles turn left (east) to continue on Cooka's Loop West. Right (south) leads to the Happy Valley Overlook, which offers a great view of the basin. Continue riding as the trail heads east and reaches the final trail junction at 5.9 miles; turn right (southeast). Left (northwest) is Cooka's Loop East. Arrive back at the Thumb Trailhead parking area at 6.0 miles.

MILES AND DIRECTIONS

0.0 Start riding north from the northwest corner of the Thumb Trailhead parking area.

0.1 Turn right (northwest) onto Cooka's Loop East. Left (west) is your return trail.

Best Bike Rides Albuquerque and Santa Fe

Galisteo Basin Preserve Trails

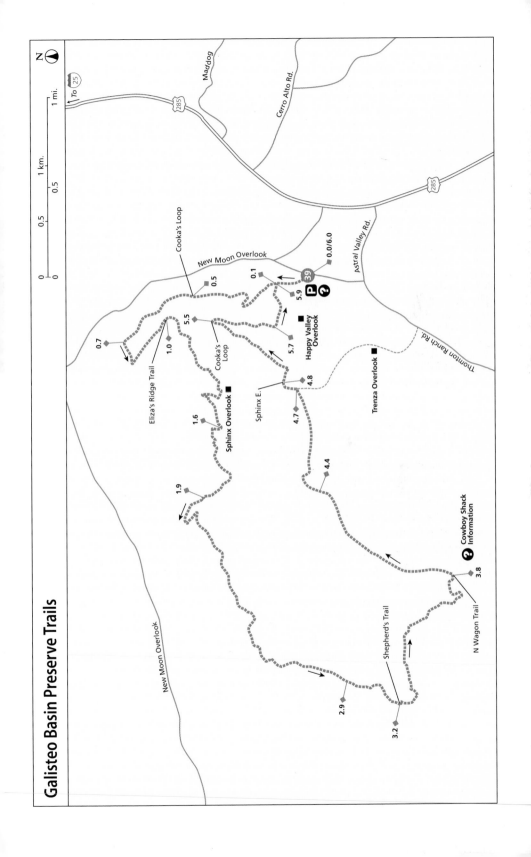

0.5 Stay right (north) on Cooka's Loop East. Left (west) shortcuts over to Cooka's Loop West.

0.7 Stay left (west) on Cooka's Loop East. Right (north) is a private trail.

1.0 Turn right (west) onto Eliza's Ridge Trail. Left (south) is Cooka's Loop West.

1.6 Cross the wash and stay to the right (north) on Eliza's Ridge Trail. Left (south) is Sphinx Loop West.

1.9 Stay straight (northwest) on Eliza's Ridge Trail. Left (south) is Cosmo's Spur; right (north) is a private trail.

2.9 Stay left (south) on Eliza's Ridge Trail. Right (north) is Sophie's Spur.

3.2 Turn left (southeast) onto the Shepherd's Trail. The Eliza's Ridge Trail continues right (southwest).

3.8 Turn left (north) onto the North Wagon Trail. Right (south) leads to the Cowboy Shack Trailhead parking area.

4.4 Stay right (northeast) on the North Wagon Trail. Left (north) is Cosmo's Spur.

4.7 Stay left (northeast) on the North Wagon Trail. Right (south) leads to the Trenza Overlook and a trail access point.

4.8 Turn right (east) onto the Sphinx Loop East. Left (northwest) is the Sphinx Loop West.

5.5 Turn right (south) onto Cooka's Loop West. Left (north), Cooka's Loop West leads back to Eliza's Ridge Trail.

5.7 Turn left (east) to continue on Cooka's Loop West. Right (south) leads to the Happy Valley Overlook.

5.9 Turn right (southeast) to return to the trailhead parking area. Left (northwest) is Cooka's Loop East.

6.0 Arrive back at the Thumb Trailhead parking area.

RIDE INFORMATION

Local Attraction
Pecos National Historic Park, 2 miles south of Pecos Village on NM 63 in Santa Fe County; (505) 757-7200; www.nps.gov/peco

Local Bike Shops
Mellow Velo Bicycles, 132 E Marcy St., Santa Fe; (505) 995-8356; www.mellow velo.com
REI, 500 Markey St., Santa Fe; (505) 982-3557; www.rei.com

Sirius Cycles Bicycle Shop, 2801 Rodeo Rd., Santa Fe; (505) 819-7311; http://sirius-cycles.com

SpinDoc, 628 Old Las Vegas Hwy., Santa Fe; (505) 819-7311; www.spindoc.com

Restaurants

Bumble Bee's Baja Grill, 301 Jefferson St., Santa Fe; (505) 820-2862; www.bumblebeesbajagrill.com

Harry's Roadhouse, 96B Old Las Vegas Hwy., Santa Fe; (505) 989-4629; www.harrysroadhousesantafe.com

Jambo Cafe, 2010 Cerrillos Rd., Santa Fe; (505) 473-1269; www.jambocafe.net

The Shed, 113½ E Palace Ave., Santa Fe; (505) 982-9030; www.sfshed.com

Cerrillos Hills State Park Trails

A trip to Cerrillos Hills State Park could satisfy several interests for some riders. A drive along the Turquoise Trail National Scenic Byway will take you through some of New Mexico's finest scenery, a few ghost towns, and even a couple of artist destinations. If the drive isn't satisfying enough, the 4.8-mile ride will take you through several rolling volcanic hills that were once successful mines for silver, iron, and lead.

Start: On the east side of CR 59, across the road from the Cerrillos Hills State Park parking area

Length: 4.8-mile loop

Riding time: 1 to 2 hours

Best bike: Mountain bike

Terrain and trail surface: Packed-dirt singletrack; sand; dirt road crossings

Traffic and hazards: Vehicles may be encountered at road crossings. Hikers also use these trails.

Maps: USGS Picture Rock and Madrid; trail map available at the trailhead and at the park office

Trail contacts: Cerrillos Hills State Park, 37 Main St., Cerrillos 87010; (505) 474-0196; www.emnrd.state.nm.us/SPD/cerrilloshillsstatepark .html

Special considerations: Rattlesnakes are present in the park.

Getting there: From Albuquerque, take I-40 East to exit 175 for NM 14/ Cedar Crest. Drive 31.9 miles on NM 14 to the turnoff for Cerrillos. Turn left (west) onto Main Street and drive 0.3 mile. Turn right (north) onto 1st Street and drive 0.6 mile to a fork in the road. Stay left at the fork onto CR 59/Camino Turquesa. Continue another 1 mile on CR 59 to the Cerrillos Hills State Park entrance and the parking area, on the left. **GPS:** N35 26.659' / W106 07.320'

THE RIDE

By linking together several of the trails in Cerrillos Hills State Park, riders can enjoy a 4.8-mile loop and discover much of what this park has to offer. The rolling hills crossed by the trails are relics of the volcanoes that were active here nearly 30 million years ago. Iron, lead, and silver were deposited here during that time. Millions of years later, Native American and Spanish explorers and settlers came here to mine those minerals as well as turquoise. The area experienced a brief and largely disappointing mining boom in the 1880s. This trail visits many of those claims and gives clues to the area's interesting human history. There are many interpretive signs along the trails, so riders hoping to learn more about the area will not be disappointed.

The hills provide a high-desert landscape of one-seed juniper, piñon pine, yucca, several species of cactus, and a diverse population of native grasses and wildflowers. Mountain lions, bobcats, coyotes, and foxes can be found in the area; look for their tracks and scat along the trail. Tarantulas also call the area home and are most likely to be spotted in early fall.

From the parking area, locate the Jane Calvin Sanchez Trail on the east side of Camino Turquesa Road. Follow the wide dirt/rock path east, then north,

Tarantulas

While many people cringe at the thought of these large hairy spiders, others find them incredibly fascinating. During mating season, September and October, it is not uncommon to find male tarantulas moving across the open desert in search of a mate. Despite their creepy appearance, tarantulas are relatively harmless. They may bite if handled, but their venom is weak and unlikely to cause long-term damage to humans. Although many claim that tarantulas prey on birds and lizards, their main food is smaller insects. Tarantulas are far from the top of the food chain, though, and many desert creatures feed on them. Tarantulas have a surprisingly long life expectancy: Females can live up to twenty years. Regardless of your feelings toward these spiders, please treat them with respect—they are an important part of this desert ecosystem.

uphill through one-seed juniper, yucca, and cacti. At 0.4 mile come to the Christian Lode Historic Mine and continue northwest. Reach the Amsterdam Rotterdam Historical Mine at 0.6 mile and continue west on the Jane Calvin Sanchez Trail. At 0.8 mile come to a T junction and turn left (west). At 1.1 miles reach Mineral Spring; continue southwest across Camino Turquesa Road.

Pick up the Escalante Trail on the opposite side of the road. This portion of the trail is fairly steep, and many will be grateful to see two rest benches—the

Trail in Cerrillos Hills State Park

first at 1.2 miles and the second at 1.3 miles. After the second bench, the trail curves sharply to the northeast. Reach an intersection with the Elkins Canyon Trail at 1.5 miles; continue north on the Escalante Trail. Come to the intersection with the Coyote Trail at 1.6 miles; continue northeast on the Escalante Trail. Shortly reach the intersection with the Cortez Mine Trail; stay north on the Escalate Trail.

A short spur trail breaks off to the left (west) at 1.7 miles. Stay north on the Escalante Trail. The trail turns sharply the left (southwest) at 1.9 miles. At 2.1 miles a spur trail to Mirador Mine breaks off to the north. Take this spur trail, which leads to one of the best viewpoints in the area at 2.2 miles. Views of Mount Taylor, the Sandia Mountains and Ortiz Mountains, Redondo Peak, Grand Central Mountain, and the Santa Fe Mountains are all available from this point (so it's worth the 0.25-mile round-trip). After taking in the spectacular views, return to the main trail at 2.3 miles.

Continue south on the Mirador Trail. At 2.5 miles come to another historic mine. This one has a footbridge over the top that gives a good view into the depths of the mine. Please be respectful and refrain from throwing anything into the mine. At 2.6 miles reach the intersection with the Coyote Trail. Turn right (south) and follow the Coyote Trail past several more historic mines and interpretive signs. Reach the intersection with the Elkins Canyon Trail at 3.1 miles. Turn right (south) onto the Elkins Canyon Trail and after about 1 mile enter a short, narrow canyon. Ride through this small canyon and reach Yerba Buena Road at 4.3 miles. The trail follows the road east for a short distance. Ride east along the road and turn north when you come to the arroyo at 4.5 miles. Ride in the arroyo for about 0.25 mile, returning to the trailhead parking area at 4.8 miles.

MILES AND DIRECTIONS

0.0   Start at the trailhead and begin riding east on the Jane Calvin Sanchez Trail.

0.4   Come to the Christian Lode Historic Mine; continue northwest.

0.6   Reach the Amsterdam Rotterdam historic mine.

0.8   Come to a T junction; turn left (west).

1.1   Reach mineral spring; continue southwest across Camino Turquesa Road and continue on the Escalante Trail.

1.2   Come to a rest bench.

1.3   Come to a second rest bench.

1.5   Intersect Elkins Canyon Trail; continue north on the Escalante Trail.

Cerrillos Hills State Park Trails

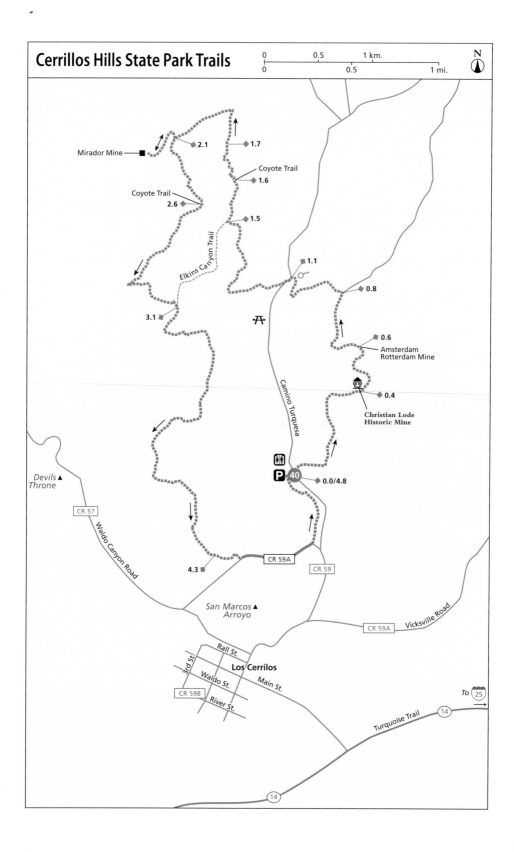

N

0   0.5   1 km.

0   0.5   1 mi.

Mirador Mine — ■

■ 2.1

◆ 1.7

Coyote Trail
◆ 1.6

Coyote Trail
2.6 ◆

◆ 1.5

Elkins Canyon Trail

◆ 1.1

◆ 0.8

3.1 ■

◆ 0.6

Amsterdam
Rotterdam Mine

◆ 0.4

Christian Lode
Historic Mine

Camino Turquesa

Devils ▲
Throne

CR 57

40   ◆ 0.0/4.8

Waldo Canyon Road

4.3 ■

CR 59A

CR 59

San Marcos ▲
Arroyo

CR 59A   Vicksville Road

Rall St.

3rd St.

Los Cerrilos

Waldo St.   Main St.

CR 59B   River St.

To 25

Turquoise Trail   14

14

1.6   Intersect Coyote Trail; continue northeast on the Escalante Trail.

1.7   Come to a spur trail; continue north on the Escalante Trail.

1.9   The trail turns sharply to the left (southwest).

2.1   Turn north on a spur trail to Mirador Mine.

2.2   Reach viewpoint; return to the Escalante Trail.

2.4   Turn south and continue on the Mirador Trail.

2.5   Come to a historic mine.

2.6   Turn right (south) onto Coyote Trail.

3.1   Turn right (south) onto Elkins Canyon Trail.

4.3   Come to Yerba Buena Road; turn left (east) and ride on the road.

4.5   Turn north (left) and ride through the arroyo.

4.8   Arrive back at the trailhead.

RIDE INFORMATION

Local Attraction

Turquoise Trail National Scenic Byway, NM 14 from Albuquerque to Santa Fe; Turquoise Trail Association; (505) 281-5233; www.turquoisetrail.org

Local Bike Shops

Mellow Velo Bicycles, 132 E Marcy St., Santa Fe; (505) 995-8356; www.mellow velo.com

REI, 500 Markey St., Santa Fe; (505) 982-3557; www.rei.com

Sirius Cycles Bicycle Shop, 2801 Rodeo Rd., Santa Fe; (505) 819-7311; http://sirius-cycles.com

SpinDoc, 628 Old Las Vegas Hwy., Santa Fe; (505) 819-7311; www.spindoc.com

Restaurants

Bumble Bee's Baja Grill, 301 Jefferson St., Santa Fe; (505) 820-2862; www.bumblebeesbajagrill.com

Harry's Roadhouse, 96B Old Las Vegas Hwy., Santa Fe; (505) 989-4629; www.harrysroadhousesantafe.com

Jambo Cafe, 2010 Cerrillos Rd., Santa Fe; (505) 473-1269; www.jambocafe.net

The Shed, 113½ E Palace Ave., Santa Fe; (505) 982-9030; www.sfshed.com

Appendix A: Land Management Agencies and Organizations

ALBUQUERQUE OPEN SPACES

Open Space Division Parks and Recreation, 3615 Los Picaros Rd. SE, Albuquerque 87105; (505) 452-5200; www.cabq.gov/openspace/riograndevalley .html

Open Space Visitor Center, 6500 Coors Blvd. NW, Albuquerque 87199; (505) 897-8831; www.cabq.gov/openspace/visitorcenter.html

BUREAU OF LAND MANAGEMENT

BLM Rio Puerco Field Office, 435 Montaño Rd. NE, Albuquerque 87107; (505) 761-8700; www.blm.gov/nm/st/en/prog/recreation/rio_puerco/perea_ nature_trail.html

FISH AND WILDLIFE SERVICE

New Mexico Department of Game and Fish—Northwest Office, 3841 Midway Place NE, Albuquerque 87109; (505) 841-8881; www.wildlife.state.nm.us/ conservation/wildlife-management-areas/

NATIONAL FORESTS

Cibola National Forest and National Grasslands, 2113 Osuna Rd. NE, Albuquerque 87113; (505) 346-3900; www.fs.usda.gov/cibola

Cibola National Forest—Sandia Ranger District, 11776 Hwy. 337, Tijeras 87059; (505) 281-3304; www.fs.usda.gov/main/cibola/home

Santa Fe National Forest, PO Box 150, Jemez Springs 87025; (505) 829-3535; www.fs.fed.us/r3/sfe/districts/jemez/visitus.html

NATIONAL MONUMENTS AND PRESERVES

Bandelier National Monument, 15 Entrance Rd., Los Alamos 87544; (505) 672-3861, ext. 517; www.nps.gov/band/index.htm

Petroglyph National Monument, 6001 Unser Blvd. NW, Albuquerque 87120; (505) 899-0205; www.nps.gov/petr/index.htm

Valles Caldera National Preserve, 39200 Hwy. 4, Jemez Springs 87025; (505) 661-3333; www.vallescaldera.gov

NEW MEXICO STATE PARKS

Cerrillos Hills State Park, 37 Main St., Cerrillos 87010; (505) 474-0196; www
.emnrd.state.nm.us/SPD/cerrilloshillsstatepark.html
Rio Grande Nature Center State Park, 2901 Candelaria Rd. NW, Albuquerque 87107; (505) 344-7240; www.emnrd.state.nm.us/SPD/riograndenature
centerstatepark.html

SANTA FE OPEN SPACE, TRAILS, AND PARKS PROGRAM

Santa Fe County, 102 Grant Ave., Santa Fe 87501-2061; (505) 986-6200; www
.santafecountynm.gov/public_works/open_space_and_trails_program

US ARMY CORPS OF ENGINEERS

Jemez Canyon Dam, 82 Dam Crest Rd., Pena Blanca 87041; (505) 465-0307;
http://corpslakes.usace.army.mil/visitors/projects.cfm?Id=L408440

Appendix B: Outdoor Recreation and Environmental Protection Groups and Organizations

Continental Divide Trail Alliance, PO Box 986, Golden, CO 80402; (303) 278-3177; www.cdtrail.org

The Continental Divide Trail Alliance is a 501-c(3) nonprofit organization with nearly 3,000 members working to increase public involvement, volunteer commitment, and private sector support on the Continental Divide Trail Alliance.

The Nature Conservancy, 212 E Marcy St., Santa Fe 87501; (505) 988-3867; www.nature.org/ourinitiatives/regions/northamerica/unitedstates/newmexico/index.htm

Over the past thirty years, The Nature Conservancy in New Mexico has worked to preserve 1.4 million acres of the state's landscapes and waterways. The organization offers field trips, events, and volunteer opportunities.

New Mexico Mountain Club, PO Box 3754, Uptown Station, Albuquerque 87190-3754; (505) 243-7767; www.nmmountainclub.org

The New Mexico Mountain Club sponsors outdoor adventures throughout the year for members and guests. They offer hiking, technical rock climbing, backpacking, camping, snowshoeing, skiing, and cycling outings.

Rails-to-Trails Conservancy, The Duke Ellington Building, 2121 Ward Ct. NW, 5th Floor, Washington, DC 20037; (202) 331-9696; www.railstotrails.org

The Rails-to-Trails Conservancy is a nonprofit organization based in Washington, DC, whose mission it is to create a nationwide network of trails from former rail lines and connecting corridors to build "healthier places for healthier people."

Sierra Club—Rio Grande Chapter, 142 Truman St. NE, Albuquerque 87108; (505) 334-3410; http://nmsierraclub.org

Since 1892 the Sierra Club has been working to protect communities, wild places, and the planet itself. The Rio Grande Chapter offers events, outings, and volunteer opportunities for conservation-minded outdoor enthusiasts.

Ride Index

About the Authors

JD Tanner grew up playing and exploring in the hills of southern Illinois. He earned a degree in outdoor recreation from Southeast Missouri State University and an advanced degree in outdoor recreation from Southern Illinois University in Carbondale. He has traveled extensively throughout the United States and is currently the director at the Touch of Nature Environmental Center at Southern Illinois University in Carbondale.

Emily Tanner grew up splitting time between southeastern Missouri and southeastern Idaho. She spent her early years fishing, hiking, and camping with her family. In college she enjoyed trying out many new outdoor activities and graduated from Southern Illinois University with an advanced degree in recreation resource administration.

Shey Lambert was born and raised in Tennessee, just outside Great Smoky Mountains National Park. The allure of the American Southwest brought him to New Mexico, where he has lived for the past several years. Shey holds a degree in outdoor leadership education and recreation from San Juan College and a degree in adventure education from Prescott College. When not out roaming in the backcountry, Shey can be found traveling, instructing outdoor leadership courses for San Juan College, and managing the High Endeavors Challenge Course facility.